Elastic Leadership

Elastic Leadership

GROWING SELF-ORGANIZING TEAMS

ROY OSHEROVE

MANNING

SHELTER ISLAND

For online information and ordering of this and other Manning books, please visit
www.manning.com. The publisher offers discounts on this book when ordered in quantity.
For more information, please contact

>Special Sales Department
>Manning Publications Co.
>20 Baldwin Road
>PO Box 761
>Shelter Island, NY 11964
>Email: orders@manning.com

Ⓜ Manning Publications Co.
20 Baldwin Road
PO Box 761
Shelter Island, NY 11964

Development editor: Christina Taylor
Review editor: Ozren Harlovic
Project editor: Tiffany Taylor
Copyeditor: Sean Gillhoolley
Proofreader: Katie Tennant
Typesetter: Dottie Marsico
Cover designer: Leslie Haimes

ISBN 9781617293085
Printed in the United States of America
1 2 3 4 5 6 7 8 9 10 – EBM – 21 20 19 18 17 16

To Tal, Itamar, Aviv, and Ido: my family.

You've taught me about
listening, challenging, and growing.

contents

preface

"There are no experts. There is only us."

These two simple sentences always make me feel lonely. They were uttered by Jeremy D. Miller, a software developer and architect I've come to appreciate over the years. These sentences give me the feeling that there's nobody else to turn to—that I have to start trusting my own instincts, and that whoever tells you they *are* an expert is either lying or wrong.

During my career, which consists of almost two decades in the IT business as of the time of this writing, I've come to realize that "There are no experts. There is only us" is very true. During one of my first jobs as a programmer, I joined a team working on a government project (the project was all in Visual Basic 6.0). The team, including my team leader, had no idea what they were doing, but because I *also* didn't know what I was doing, I *assumed* that whatever people were doing was the right way to do it.

As time went by, I began to read books about how software development *could* work, including *The Mythical Man-Month* by Fred Brooks (University of North Carolina at Chapel Hill, 1974) and *Peopleware* by Tom DeMarco and Timothy Lister (Dorset House Publishing, 1987). I looked around and recognized all the problems those books were talking about right there in front of me.

But nobody around me said anything about the crap we were building or the crap we were taking from our managers and customers, and *certainly* nobody said *anything* about the crap we were giving to our customers and managers—there was only silence. Nobody was talking about careless, helpless programmers. Everything was *fine*. To paraphrase (and counter) a famous saying by comedian Louis C.K., "Everything was crappy, and nobody cared."

These were *good people*. Some were my friends, and they didn't intend to do any harm. We were doing our best, in the same way ants do their best to vanquish raindrops along their path to the anthill. But we weren't looking *up*. We weren't trying to understand and predict *why* the rain fell or where it falls from. We didn't plan better ways to get to the anthill, and we didn't get better raincoats to protect ourselves from the rain (OK, ant raincoats are a sign this analogy is breaking down, so I'll stop).

We were all just *there*, doing our ant-like jobs. Project late? Sure; that's life. Quality is lousy? Sure; that's life. Debugging until 3 a.m.? Sure; that's normal.

Was I the only one reading books? No. There weren't many trade books, but there were *some*. But the books my coworkers were reading weren't getting them anywhere; or if the books had the potential to help them, maybe they couldn't find the time to finish the books and get there.

There was no sense of craftsmanship. But there was also no sense of professionalism. There were just big downward spirals for every project, as far as the eye could see.

This workplace wasn't unique, by any means. I encountered many companies like this, with variations, over the years. I hate working at places like that; I always want to make a difference.

This book is about making a difference and getting other people to make a difference as well. It's the book for those who feel hopelessly trapped in their jobs, even though they're architects, scrum masters, team leaders, or senior developers. It's the book I wish I'd had when I first became a team leader.

The book started out as a passionate blog that I kept over several years at 5whys.com (now ElasticLeadership.com). At some point, I collected all the blog posts and published them in a self-published book at leanpub.com titled *Notes to a Software Team Leader*. When Manning offered to publish it a couple of years later, I jumped at the chance to revise and add content to the book and publish it with the same company that helped publish my first book, *The Art of Unit Testing*. I'd like to thank Manning for helping me publish this new edition of *Notes to a Software Team Leader*, now titled *Elastic Leadership* and with a new format and new and updated content.

acknowledgments

I'd like to thank Kevlin Henney for coming up with the idea for the original title of this book, which was *Notes to a Software Team Leader*. Later I changed the title because the book now included more than just notes, but that spirit remains in the second part of the book. You can reach Kevlin at www.curbralan.com.

Thank you, early beta reviewers of this book's original digital edition—especially Ofer Zelig, Leif Eric Fredheim, Mauricio Diazorlich, and Eric Potter—for providing many insightful and helpful ideas and corrections.

A big thank goes you to the early purchasers of this book when it was still in its infancy at leanpub.com, before it was picked up by Manning. *They* are the reason this book was finished. And thank you leanpub .com for showing another way to write a book in a lean/agile way.

Thank you, the people at Manning: publisher Marjan Bace and everyone on the editorial and production teams, including Janet Vail, Mary Piergies, Tiffany Taylor, Dottie Marsico, Sean Gillhoolley, Katie Tennant, and many others who worked behind the scenes.

Finally, thanks go to the amazing group of technical peer reviewers led by Ozren Harlovic: Matt Belanger, Jeroen Benckhuijsen, Art Bergquist, Ali Berkol, Alessandro Campeis, Maria Gemini, Karl Geoghegan, Christopher Haupt, Andy Kirsch, Edgar Knapp, Antti Koivisto, Shaun Lippy, Sune Lomholt, Ashwin Mhatre, Tim Moore, Ferdinando Santacroce, Jonathan Sharley, Ivo Štimac, and Ian de Villiers.

about this book

This book has the following goals:

- Inspire would-be team leaders to take the plunge
- Teach new and experienced leaders how to deal with everyday issues that are people-related
- Explore a new manifesto and value system for leaders to follow, and use as a compass when making tough decisions
- Teach leaders how to teach others and how to learn new skills themselves through challenges

Who should read this book

Although this book is primarily written from the viewpoint of someone who works in the software industry, I've heard from people in other industries that the concepts in the book have helped them as well. Anyone in a leadership position (present or future) may find value here; and people in the software industry will find most of the concepts relatable.

This book is intended for anyone who has thought about undertaking or is currently in a leadership position. This isn't limited to managers or team leads. If you're in any position in which you make decisions that other people rely on and wait for, this book can help you learn how to improve your professional life and the professional lives of the people around you. People who fit into this category may include software architects, build managers, security folks, UI experts, and more. If you have the word *expert* in your job title, it's very likely you can find value in this book.

Roadmap

The elastic leadership model is introduced in chapters 1–10. Then, in chapters 11–32, I've assembled a plethora of notes from new and experienced leaders and consultants about leadership do's and don'ts. I've also added my own interpretation of where their advice fits into the elastic leadership model and manifesto:

- *Part 1*—Chapter 1 introduces the overall value system and manifesto this book follows. Everything else ties into parts of this chapter. Chapters 2 and 3 discuss the concepts of elastic leadership and bus factors, and how to use the value system in real life in what I call the *elastic leadership model.* Bus factors represent the first low-hanging fruit that can be changed when you look at your environment.
- *Part 2*—Chapter 4 deals with *survival mode,* the first of the three modes of operation under the elastic leadership model. Many teams are in survival mode, and the hardest thing about this mode is that it's usually a downward spiral: things tend to get progressively worse when you try to fix them. This chapter discusses how you can get out of this mode and move on to learning mode.
- *Part 3*—Chapters 5–7 deal with *learning mode,* which is the second of the three modes. Chapter 5 discusses how learning happens (mostly through ravines). Chapter 6 talks about commitment language and how it helps to bring up issues that people may not be comfortable talking about with you. We'll move to challenging teams into ravines in chapter 7—a key technique for successful leaders, which can also be a double-edged sword if abused.
- *Part 4*—Chapters 8–10 deal with *self-organization mode*: how to measure it and how to cultivate it. These chapters discuss the role of the leader in this mode and how to set up special clearing meetings that help expose team issues (these are not retrospectives, but deeper conversations). You'll also learn about influence patterns.

- *Part 5*—Chapters 11–32 present an assortment of notes from people I've asked to contribute, each with an analysis by me regarding how it ties in with the manifesto in chapter 1.

About the author

Roy Osherove is the DevOps process lead for the West Coast at Dell EMC, based in California. He is also the author of *The Art of Unit Testing* (Manning, 2013) and *Enterprise DevOps* (http://enterprisedevops .org). He consults and trains teams worldwide on the gentle art of leadership, unit testing, test-driven development, and continuous-delivery automation. He frequently speaks at international conferences on these topics and others.

You can find more information at these sites:

- ElasticLeadership.com—The blog that started this book
- Osherove.com—Roy's other blog
- Osherove Online Training (courses.osherove.com)—Roy's online training on TDD, DevOps, and, soon, elastic leadership

Author Online

Purchase of *Elastic Leadership* includes free access to a private web forum run by Manning Publications where you can make comments about the book, ask technical questions, and receive help from the author and from other users. To access the forum and subscribe to it, point your web browser to www.manning.com/books/ elastic-leadership. This page provides information on how to get on the forum once you are registered, what kind of help is available, and the rules of conduct on the forum.

Manning's commitment to our readers is to provide a venue where a meaningful dialog between individual readers and between readers and the author can take place. It is not a commitment to any specific amount of participation on the part of the author, whose contribution to the forum remains voluntary (and unpaid). We suggest you try asking him some challenging questions lest his interest stray! The Author Online forum and the archives of previous discussions will be accessible from the publisher's website as long as the book is in print.

About the cover

The figure on the cover of *Elastic Leadership* is captioned "Le légumier," or "A gardener." Much like a gardener who grows and tends plants in the right conditions, a good leader knows when to sow, when to water, and when to let go.

The illustration is taken from a nineteenth-century edition of Sylvain Maréchal's four-volume compendium of regional dress customs published in France. Each illustration is finely drawn and colored by hand. The rich variety of Maréchal's collection reminds us vividly of how culturally apart the world's towns and regions were just 200 years ago. Isolated from each other, people spoke different dialects and languages. In the streets or in the countryside, it was easy to identify where they lived and what their trade or station in life was just by what they were wearing.

Dress codes have changed since then, and the diversity by region, so rich at the time, has faded away. It's now hard to tell apart the inhabitants of different continents, let alone different towns or regions. Perhaps we have traded cultural diversity for a more varied personal life—certainly for a more varied and fast-paced technological life.

At a time when it's hard to tell one computer book from another, Manning celebrates the inventiveness and initiative of the computer business with book covers based on the rich diversity of regional life of two centuries ago, brought back to life by Maréchal's pictures.

Part 1

Understanding
elastic leadership

You can't depend on your eyes when your imagination is out of focus.
—Mark Twain

Chapter 1 introduces this book's overall value system and manifesto; everything in the book ties in with this first chapter. Chapter 2 discusses the concepts of elastic leadership and how to use the book's value system in real life in what I call the elastic leadership model. Chapter 3 talks about bus factors—the first low-hanging fruit that can be changed to improve your work environment.

1

Striving toward a
Team Leader Manifesto

The reasonable man adapts himself to the world; the unreasonable one persists in trying to adapt the world to himself. Therefore all progress depends on the unreasonable man.

—George Bernard Shaw,
Man and Superman

This chapter covers

- *Principles of leadership*
- *How to become and remain a good leader*
- *Developing other leaders from your peers—growing people*

This chapter outlines the principles for becoming, and remaining, a good leader, and also developing other leaders from among your peers.

Leadership in general—and team leadership in the software business in particular, where little training, if any, is provided—isn't easy to accomplish, or indeed to measure. We can begin with the assumption that most people in software—like you—have no idea what they're

3

doing or what they should be looking at when leading their software teams. Yes, that was me too.

This book springs from my personal experience of what *worked* for me and what *didn't* work for me when I was leading software teams.

One thing is certain: the way we work with our teams must improve. We must become better adjusted to the current reality and needs of our team, our business, and ourselves.

A few years ago, I was speaking at a programming conference. The person who introduced me also mentioned that I was looking for a job. At the end of the talk, a woman came up to me and said, "We want to hire you as a developer." Boy, was I proud of myself that day. I began working there, and the woman became my team leader.

My first job was to write code that uses the local network and searches for specific data on remote hard drives (no, it was not a virus). I worked on it alone. As the day went on, I struggled and struggled. It was harder than I thought. Another day came and went, and I was still at it. My ego wouldn't let me ask for help. They had hired me off a conference stage because I was supposed to be an expert. How bad would I look if I said I didn't know how to solve this problem—the *first* problem I had been given at that job? No. I was determined to work on it until I figured it out.

To add to my grief, there were no daily stand-ups, and every few days my team leader would pass by me and ask lightly how things were going. I would deliberately say it was "in progress" and move on with a solemn face. A week went by and I began avoiding people's eyes in the hallways. I pretended to be busy and pensive, but I was drowning inside. Every day that went by, it became harder to admit I was stuck. Every day that went by made it harder to ask for help; I would look more stupid with the little progress I had made during all that time.

At some point, I took sick leave for a few days. I couldn't handle the silent pressure. When I came back from the leave, my team leader approached me and said, "Hey, by the way, that thing you were working on? One of the devs and I sat on it and made it work in a few hours." They had found a simple way out of my mess, and I felt both betrayed and foolish. I was fired from that company shortly after with a budget-cut excuse, but I knew better.

There were many things that could have prevented this Greek tragedy:

- I could have been a bit more courageous and said, "I don't know how to fix this," early on.
- We could have had daily stand-ups where my predicament would have been discovered early.
- We could have had a rule whereby no one was allowed to work on something on their own for more than a day.
- My team leader could have approached me and done one-on-one meetings weekly or biweekly to discover what was up.

But nothing happened, until the worst happened.

The values I introduce here, and throughout this book, can help prevent such tragedies from transpiring, or at least make them very unlikely. I hope they can help spark a desire in you, the reader, to become better at what you do.

Why should you care?

You might feel helpless in leading your team to do the things you believe to be "right." This book can help.

You might feel like you want to keep your head above water. This book will help you accomplish much more. You might feel clueless as to what it is you're supposed to be doing with your (future) team. We'll tackle that too. You might be broken and scared because you have no idea how you're going to get out of a bad situation at work. Welcome to the club. I hope I can help. I hope I can because I've been there—clueless and scared. I was lucky enough to have some good mentors along the way who challenged me to do the things that I was afraid to do, to get out of my comfort zone, and to learn things I didn't even know I didn't know.

I think team leaders around the world all suffer from some of the same basic bad experiences. Most of us weren't taught how to do this type of work, and most of us are never going to get mentors to help us through it. Maybe what we're all missing are some good, old-fashioned people skills. Maybe we're missing some direction, some overall purpose for our leadership role. I feel that if we go uninformed into a leadership role in software, without a sense of purpose and strategy, we've already lost the battle to create real teams. Yes, our head might be above water, but are we there to slog through another day? Are we supposed to be this helpless? We want to be *leaders* who create not only real value but also happy teams, both fulfilled and loyal.

Don't be afraid to become management

A lot of developers who are promoted to leaders, or who are offered the opportunity to become team leaders, seem to be resistant to becoming management. I can understand some of the reasoning, but I don't accept it. You might be afraid that your time will be sucked up by meetings, that you won't have time to do the things you love the most (like coding), and that you might lose friendships with people you currently work with. I agree that there's a basis for those fears. We've all seen (or been) that person who doesn't have time to do what they love, or fumbles a friendship because they've turned into a boss from hell, and so on.

Paraphrasing Jerry Weinberg in his book *Managing Teams Congruently* (Weinberg & Weinberg, 2011): Management, done wrong, can make these fears manifest into reality. But management done right negates them. Management, done right, is a very tough job. That's why you get paid more.

I'll return to this concept later in this book.

You can make time for the things you care about

A good leader will challenge the team and the people around them to solve their own problems, instead of solving everyone's problems for them. As people gradually learn to solve their own problems, your time frees up more and more to do the things you care more about, and the things that matter more (sitting down with people, coding to keep in sync with what's going on in the team and the code). Doing your job as a leader and challenging or asking people to accomplish tasks may indeed feel weird, but in my experience, doing it will garner *more* respect for you, not less. Yes, some things will change, but change is inevitable. You might as well own and control how things change.

It also takes time to challenge people, time that most teams don't have in abundance. Making slack time to grow the team's skills will be necessary.

Take the opportunity to learn new, exciting things every day

Nothing beats gaining new skills. You and your team should always be getting better and going out of your comfort zone to learn new things. This is essential to what a team leader does. Becoming a team leader requires personal growth, rising to the challenge of knowing your team and what you can expect from them.

Experiment with human beings

Yes. I said it. You have a team, and you can experiment with goals, constraints, and the different leadership styles described in this book. Experimenting is one of the most enjoyable and interesting things I love about being a leader.

Be more than one thing

You're not only a developer; you're also a leader. You can change things that bother you and do things that you think are right. How many times have you said to yourself, "I wish I could change X?" As a leader, you can do something about it. If you choose not to become a manager, you'll have far less influence. As my friend Jeremy Miller said,

> *There are no experts. There is only us.*

As you may have noticed in the preface to this book, I think that statement is spot on. Sometimes you must be the person who gets up and does something. You'll be surprised by how many people will follow you. Remember that 90% of success is stepping up to the plate.

Challenge yourself and your team

I've heard this basic idea expressed in a couple of different ways:

- Do one thing every day that scares you. (Eleanor Roosevelt)
- Get rejected at least once a day (also known as "Rejection Therapy").

These ideas are powerful and good ways to make sure you're learning something. I believe that learning something truly new is neither easy nor simple. In fact, many times it's scary, annoying, or discouraging enough to make you want to give up halfway through the challenge. Leadership, done right, can be difficult to learn. But as you make progress, you'll be amazed by your growth. You won't be the same person you were before embarking on this journey.

When you read the words *great challenge*, what comes to mind?

Depending on your state of mind, *great challenge* can be taken either gravely ("I'm facing an awful great challenge") or enthusiastically ("Wow, great challenge!"). Choose the second option.

The following section may present a *great challenge* to you.

The Team Leader Manifesto

This manifesto is continuously being developed and refined. You can find the latest version of it at http://5whys.com/manifesto. The high aspirations of the manifesto can be seen in figure 1.1.

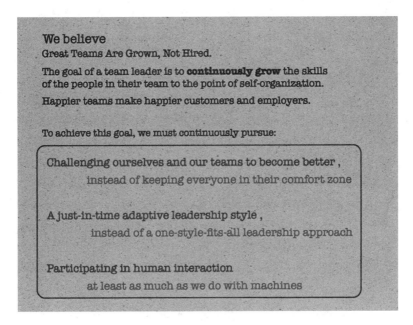

We believe

Great Teams Are Grown, Not Hired.

The goal of a team leader is to **continuously grow** the skills of the people in their team to the point of self-organization.

Happier teams make happier customers and employers.

To achieve this goal, we must continuously pursue:

Challenging ourselves and our teams to become better ,
    instead of keeping everyone in their comfort zone

A just-in-time adaptive leadership style ,
    instead of a one-style-fits-all leadership approach

Participating in human interaction
    at least as much as we do with machines

Figure 1.1   The Team Leader Manifesto

Here's a breakdown of the manifesto, line by line.

For us as team leaders, the goal and the way we measure our success is through the overall growth in skills of self-organization and self-maintenance in each member of our team, and in the team as a whole.

To that end:

- We accept that what the team needs from us changes continuously based on their skills for handling the reality of work, and we embrace a continuously changing leadership style over a one-style-fits-all approach.
- We believe in challenging ourselves and our teams to always improve; therefore:
  - We create slack time for the team to learn and be challenged.

- We embrace taking risks for our team over staying safe.
- We embrace fear and discomfort while learning new skills over keeping people within their comfort zone.
- We embrace experimentation as a constant practice over maintaining the status quo
  - With people
  - With tools
  - With processes
  - With the work environment
- We believe our core practice is leading people, not wielding machines; therefore:
  - We embrace spending more time with our team than in meetings.
  - We embrace treating software problems as people problems.
  - We learn people skills and communication techniques.

Next up

The most important thing you'll need to know before you plan how to lead is the three team phases: survival mode, learning mode, and self-organization, which the next chapter discusses.

Summary

Leadership is a challenging thing to accept. If we don't accept it, there are others who will, who might not do justice to the power they wield.

There are many benefits to becoming a leader, including learning a new set of skills, becoming more valuable to the organization, and experiencing a greater feeling of accomplishment.

Sadly, many people take on a leadership role and don't know what to do with it, and they feel overwhelmed. This book is my way of contributing to help prevent that from happening.

Team leaders are the first line of defense (or attack) in making things work from the ground up. Without their help, an organization will be stuck spinning its wheels in neutral forever, no matter how hard upper management presses on the gas.

Without the leadership skills and practices outlined in the chapters that follow, it's hard to make positive changes in the work environment.

2

Matching leadership styles to team phases

This chapter covers

- *Three team phases*
- *Leadership types*
- *Goals for team leaders*

This chapter is a quick guide to recognizing the three team phases and the leadership types that make the most sense for each phase.

First, let's clarify *why* we need to define these phases. The reasons have to do with our overall goal as team leaders. What do *you* think your role is as a team leader? For a few years, I had to guess. Nobody told me and I had no one to learn from.

Before we go on, I want to clarify the terms used in this book. The words *phase* and *mode* are used almost interchangeably throughout the book. For example, in the *learning phase* you go into *learning mode*. *Phase* is where you think your team is; *mode* is how you react to which phase you're in. Think of it like the fight-or-flight instincts that we all have. When these instincts take over, we act a certain way. So you might say that when we recognize we are in the survival phase, we initiate our survival instinct or survival mode. Or if we recognize that we're operating in learning mode while our organization is operating in survival mode, we can say we're in a survival phase and we should initiate survival mode behavior and instinct.

The role of the team leader

In the past, one of my biggest mistakes as a team leader was that I didn't recognize that my style of leadership was oblivious to the needs of my team.

Initially, my idea of what a team leader should do went something like this: a team leader should provide their team everything the team needs and then get out of their way.

Boy, did I think I was stellar! When people needed something—working code, infrastructure, a faster machine, or an answer to something—I was their guy. By my own definition back then, I was doing a great job. But that meant that I had little time for myself and was mostly in meetings or coding all day. I didn't allow myself to take even a couple of days to go on a vacation. I was always at work because people needed me. And it felt great to be needed.

Looking back, I can see lots of room for improvement, because the role of a team leader is vastly different from solving problems and getting out of the way.

Growth through challenge

Here's what I believe my role is today: a team leader helps develop quality people on the team.

I believe this should be your first "compass" in determining your behavior as a lead. You may ask, "What about delivering value to the company?" I believe that delivering value flows naturally from developing your team's skills. When people grow, value delivery also grows because skills grow. More importantly, the attachment and commitment of people to do the right thing also grows. Loyalty grows.

One of my mentors, Eli Lopian, told me this once:

> *People don't quit their jobs. They quit their managers.*

I think that's a true statement (at least for the several companies I've quit). By coaching the people on your team to develop as team players or valuable working individuals, you generate internal value for them personally, not only for the company. True loyalty comes when you have everything to gain by sticking around and you realize it.

Challenge

More things logically follow if your guiding rule is to help people grow. To grow people at work means to help them acquire new skills. For them to acquire skills, you must challenge them. Therefore, you have to stop solving all their problems for them and coach them to solve problems on their own (with your guidance). If you solve all problems for your team, the only person learning how to do new things is you.

You're the bottleneck

When you solve all your team's problems, you're the bottleneck, and they'll find themselves unable to manage without you. If you're sick for three days, can you leave your phone turned off? Or are you constantly worried and logging in to the company's VPN to check and fix things that nobody else on the team can do? If the team has to wait for you to be available to solve problems, you're the bottleneck, and you'll never have time to do the things that matter most.

Crunch time and leadership styles

You might think, "Well, that makes no sense. We're in crunch time! The release is late, and now I'm supposed to take what little time we have left to teach people new things? I have enough on my plate as it is!" And you'd be right. It's not always a good idea to start challenging people. Sometimes, challenges don't make sense.

Challenging people is *one* style of leadership. Let's talk about two more:

- *Command-and-control* leadership
- *Facilitating* leadership

Why do we need to talk about the other styles? Because *challenging* to encourage growth isn't always a good idea. I know it sounds crazy and is contrary to the advice of agilists, but hear me out. Sometimes, a command-and-control style of leadership is required, especially in survival mode, as we'll discuss in the next few chapters.

Command and control is sometimes a good idea because there are times when a team leader must be able to direct their team down a path where the team has no time to learn the skills needed to deal with the current circumstances (such as when fighting many fires).

The third leadership style, *facilitation*, is described by many agile consultants this way: "Lock the team in a room, give them a goal, and get the hell out of their way." Agile methodologies sometimes call this a "self-organizing" team.

Facilitation is a good idea sometimes, if the team already knows how to do the work and solve their own problems. A command-and-control leader would get in the way of getting the job done.

Which leadership style should you choose?

It seems like the previously discussed approaches—challenge, command-and-control, and facilitation—are good styles at different points in time. Team leaders have succeeded by doing each, but many have failed with each as well. When *does* it make sense to use each of these different leadership ideas? When are the times that, as a leader, you need to take charge and start making hard decisions? When will using command-and-control leadership hurt more than it helps?

When should you lock your team in a room and get out of their way because they know what they're doing?

I'll recap the three different leadership types that I've seen in the wild:

- Challenging/coaching leader
- Command-and-control leader
- Facilitating leader (self-organizing teams)

It's easier for me to start with an answer to an opposing question: "When should I *not* use each leadership style?"

Let's examine each one in turn and see when each can result in negative consequences.

Command and control

We have all seen or been this type of leader at some point. You tell people what to do. You are the "decider." You take one for the team, but you also have the team in your pocket in terms of hierarchy, decision-making, and control over everyone's actions.

The command-and-control leader might also try to solve everyone's problems. I once had a team leader who, my first day on the team, set up my laptop while typing blazingly fast on the keyboard and not sharing with me anything he was doing. When I asked questions, he muttered something along the lines of "Don't concern yourself with this now. You have more important things to do." (Read that sentence with a heavy Russian accent for better effect.)

With a controlling leader, there's little room for people to learn, take sole ownership, or take initiative that might go against the rules. The consequences are too undesirable.

The command-and-control approach won't work if your team already knows what they're doing or if they expect to learn new things and be challenged to become better.

Coach

The coach is also known as "the teacher" and is great at teaching new things to others. The opposite of the controlling leader, the coach is great at teaching others to make decisions while letting them make the wrong decisions as long as there's an important lesson to be learned.

Time is not an issue for a coach, because learning requires time. It's like teaching your kid to put on their shoes and tie their shoelaces—it takes time, but it's an important skill, and you'd be making a mistake not taking the time to let your kid go through this exercise on their own, cheering them from the sidelines.

The coaching approach won't work if you and your team don't have enough free time to practice and do any learning. If you're busy putting out fires all day, and you're already behind schedule anyway, you won't have time to also learn or try new things like refactoring or test-driven development.

Facilitator

The facilitator stays out of everyone's way. Whereas the coach challenges people to stop and learn something, the facilitator makes sure that the current environment, conditions, goals, and constraints are such that they will drive the team to get things done. The facilitator doesn't solve the team's problems but instead relies on the team's existing skills to solve their own problems.

The facilitator approach won't work if the team doesn't have sufficient skills to solve their own problems (such as slow machines, customer demands, and so on).

Now that we've discussed circumstances that are unfavorable for each leadership style, let's talk about when they're most effective.

Leadership styles and team phases

Each of these leadership types belongs in a different phase of the team's needs. There are times when a team needs a commander, times when it needs a coach, and times when it needs a facilitator. I call them the *three team phases.*

A beta tester for the book commented that the word *phase* gives him a bad vibe "due to bad memories on some poorly managed, waterfall-style projects." I'm still not sure what to call these things myself. *States* might be better suited, but I'm still debating this. If you have a better name for what I call team phases, email me at roy@osherove.com (or through contact.osherove.com) with the subject "Naming Phases."

The three team phases

These phases are how I decide which leadership type is required for the current team (see figure 2.1). The question "Which leadership type is right?" should be asked on a daily basis because teams can flow in and out of these phases based on many factors.

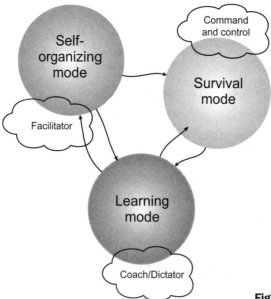

Figure 2.1   The three team phases

Survival phase (no time to learn)

Survival sounds dramatic and is as alarming as it sounds. It doesn't necessarily mean coffee-stained carpets and a sleepless staff. I define survival as *your team not having enough time to learn.*

In order to accomplish your goal as a leader (coaching people to grow), you need to make time to learn, and your main strategy, or instinct during this phase, is to *get the team out of the survival phase by creating slack time.* In order to get slack time, you'll most likely need to use a command-and-control style of leadership.

Learning phase (learning to solve your own problems)

You can tell you're in the learning phase when *your team has enough slack time to learn and experiment and you're using that slack time.*

Slack time can be used for learning new skills, removing technical debt, or, better yet, doing both at the same time:

- Learning and gradually implementing test-driven development, with people who have no experience
- Enhancing or building a continuous integration cycle, with people who have no experience
- Enhancing test coverage, with people who have no experience
- Learning about and refactoring code, with people who have no experience

In short, use slack time to do anything constructive, and tack on the phrase "with people who have no experience" at the end of the sentence.

Your main goal as a leader (in order to achieve your overall role of growing people) is to *grow the team to be self-organizing by teaching and challenging them to solve their own problems.*

In order to achieve that, you need to become more of a coaching leader, with the occasional intervention of the controlling leader for those cases when you don't have enough slack time to learn from a specific mistake.

Self-organizing phase (facilitate, experiment)

You can tell you're in the self-organizing phase if *you can leave work for a few days without being afraid to turn off your cell phone and laptop.* If you can do that, come back, and find that things are going well, your team is in the unique position of solving their own problems without your help.

Your goal in the self-organizing phase is to keep things as they are by being a facilitator, and keep a close eye on the team's ability to handle the current reality. When the team's dynamics change, you can determine which leadership style you need to use next.

The self-organizing phase is also a lot of fun because this is the phase where you have the most time to experiment and try different approaches, constraints, and team goals that will develop your team.

This is the point where you have time to do the things that matter most. As a leader, you have a vision. If you're always keeping your head down, you can't look up and see if your team is going in the right direction.

From my personal experience, most of the teams I've seen are far from self-organizing. My belief (though I have little more than gut feeling and anecdotal experience) is that maybe 5% of software teams *in the world* are truly self-organizing and are capable of solving their own problems. Some 80% of the software teams out there are probably in survival mode. How often have you been part of a team that kept putting out fires and never had time to do "the right thing"?

How do you switch to a different phase?

When does a team move between phases?

It's important that you recognize when your team needs a new type of leadership, and you'll have to keep a close eye on the team's

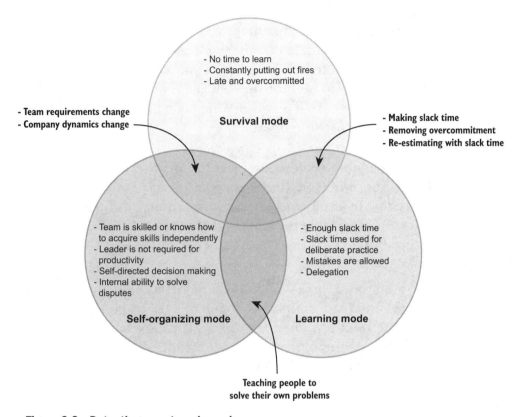

Figure 2.2 Detecting your team's mode

main assets; see figure 2.2. Any event that can shift the balance of the following team assets can cause the team to have different needs from you as a leader:

- Asset #1: The team's knowledge and skill to solve their own problems
- Asset #2: The team's amount of slack time

Here are examples of events that could trigger a team phase shift:

- *You bring into the team new people who lack the skills to solve their own problems.*   You might be going into the learning phase. If they still have *time* to learn, then you are indeed in the learning mode. You can use this time to teach those problem-solving skills to the new team members. Better yet, you might take the opportunity to teach some of the more experienced folks on the team how to mentor the new team members to solve their own problems. That way everyone is challenged and growing, not only the new members.

- *You or someone else is changing deadlines on known goals.*   This could possibly remove any slack time the team is using to learn. You might be in the survival phase. Time to get out of there fast by removing some commitments and making more slack time available for learning!

Next up

This chapter was a quick walk-through of recognizing the three team phases and leadership types that make the most sense for each phase. In the next few chapters, I'll go through each of the team phases, diving deeply into the specific leadership styles and techniques that have proved effective for me.

Summary

- The role of the team leader is to grow the people on their team. This growth is the overall compass through which the leader should navigate important decisions. To grow, the team must first have time to practice new skills and make mistakes; slack time is necessary.

- In survival mode, there's no time to learn, and the leader helps make time for the team. In the learning phase, the leader coaches the team and helps them grow; and in the self-organization phase, the leader acts more as a facilitator, letting the team move on without much interference.

- A team can move between the states rapidly based on the current reality and makeup of the team.

3

Dealing with bus factors

This chapter covers

- *Bus factors and why they inhibit leadership*
- *How to remove bus factors*
- *How to avoid bus factors*

Before I explore survival mode later in this book, I want to discuss one of the primary reasons for finding yourself in this mode. Bus factors are ubiquitous, and they're a huge risk to your projects.

Bus factors

A bus factor can be defined this way: the number of people who need to get hit by a bus for the project or team to stop functioning. Therefore, a bus factor of *one* is the riskiest.

If you've worked in the software industry for any length of time, ask yourself, "Do I know a person in my project who, if they disappeared tomorrow, would leave the project or team stuck?" It's unlikely you can provide multiple names.

These people (roles) are examples of bus factors. I had a friend who joked that "every successful software company is hiding a "Yuri" (referring to a Russian who is likely a genius) in the basement who does all the important stuff." Joking aside, "Yuri" represents someone who knows things most people do not, and the company hangs on their word to accomplish a specific task. Many companies have multiple "Yuris." They're a huge risk (no matter where they were born, or what accent they have or don't have).

Let's break down some of the reasons they're a risk:

- They're a single point of failure.
- They create a bottleneck that slows things to a crawl.
- They can reduce morale and induce job insecurity.
- They discourage team growth.

A single point of failure

I once consulted at a large insurance provider. One of the projects, with about 200 developers, had only one build consultant, an outside consultant who had been working with them for several years. His job was to take care of the build and release. A release took a week. There was one release every month.

Everyone stayed out of each other's way, and he minded his own business as well, keeping his head down in his lane.

One day he got tired of working at the same place on the same project and transferred to a different consulting gig at another place. The project (the company's main source of revenue) was unable to release any software *at all.* No bug fixes to production, no new features seeing the light of day. Nothing. This meant a huge monetary loss, as the well as possible loss of new customers.

Everyone was running around like headless chickens, trying to fix this. Eventually they called the build consultant and paid him three times his usual hourly rate to sit there for a couple of weeks, while they attached a mic and screen-recording software to his machine. He did two consecutive releases (a fake one and a real one). They were lucky he was still available, but they paid a lot of money to mitigate that risk.

Lesson: The fewer people you have who know an important part of your business, the more you will pay when they move on.

A bottleneck that slows things to a crawl

One of the large projects I consulted for had a huge problem with code quality and slow release cycles. Nobody knew why the quality was so low. All they knew was that they wanted to fix it, so I paired with the developers for a few days, and things became clear.

One developer was working on a long function that was unreadable and unmaintainable. He was adding spaghetti code to spaghetti code.

When I asked him why he wouldn't refactor his new code a little bit or extract to an external method, his reply was, "That'd be crazy. If I do that, I'm going to have to ask for a new code review for that code section, and those things take days until they're done by an architect."

Interesting. I went to see the architects. Turns out there were only two architects who were allowed to do code reviews, and they were usually busy writing new code, as their boss directed. They had little time to review code changes and approve them. Even getting code into a regular development source control branch could take days, which slowed the place down to a crawl.

A bottleneck like that makes it hard to keep up with fixes, add changes quickly, or even show demos and get feedback fast enough in a sprint cycle.

> **NOTE** In the language of the theory of constraints, a bus factor is a type of constraint, and everything will move as slowly as the slowest constraint.

Reducing morale and inducing job insecurity

There are negative consequences for the person who is the bus factor. Time for another true story!

I once consulted at a large software/hardware firm. The build process was managed by three people, and they were extremely defensive about teaching people how to use the build process. One of them was adamantly against showing other people how the build worked, because he felt it was *his* job. He was *the* specialist with 20 years of training on the job.

It can be said that being the only expert is a good way to have job security, but it's a double-edged sword. An organization will (eventually) seek to reduce the bus factor risk, whether they know what to call it or not. Sometimes it takes longer to get the wheels rolling on that endeavor. A person who's a bus factor and avoids reducing the factor will usually have to take a forceful stand against the organization, effectively holding the project or team hostage, because no one else can fill their role.

The organization is likely to try to find the first "match" to come along to replace or augment that person's job to reduce the bus factor. The more forceful they were originally, the less chance they have of staying on if someone with the same, or better, skill set who is also a team player comes along.

In short, if you're enjoying a monopoly, you can't wait to jump ship the moment a merely adequate competitor comes along.

Discouraging team growth

I've seen many people quit their jobs because they weren't learning anything new. They got bored doing the same work and not being challenged, and they moved on to more challenging pastures.

Bus factors are knowledge silos by definition, and knowledge silos that aren't broken can lead to the "not my job" mentality (Google "Not my Job Award" to view other examples).

In that atmosphere, even people who want to learn and be challenged will have a hard time finding new challenges because they're expected to stay in their own little cube (like that company with the build consultant). That, in turn, makes for a team of specialists, or, to put it more bluntly, a team of *bus factors.*

I have a true story that demonstrates this problem.

One of the places I consulted for had an issue: the search server was failing, and because it was set up by an external company, nobody on the team knew how to fix it. The people from the external consultancy were on a company vacation or something of that sort, and they would have taken at lease three days to fix the problem.

Here's how it was fixed. A developer called the expert on the phone (during their vacation), and the expert told the developer exactly what to type into the terminal.

The developer *blindly* typed the commands into the terminal, waited, then said, "Okay, it seems to work now," and hung up. I was there, listening, and was sad to see this.

What a *huge* wasted opportunity to learn something that might help solve this problem next time. Not even *"Why did that command fix it?"* or *"Why did it fail? What can we do next time on our own to prevent this?"*

This is what that mentality begets: lots of lost time, and people putting cubicles inside their minds, discouraging learning.

Removing bus factors

I've used several ways to remove existing bus factors in the past. Some of them are gradual but more effective in the long run. Others are faster but a bit less effective in the long run.

Pairing and coaching

Ask the bus factor to pair up for at least 30 minutes a day with one other person in the team. During that time, let the less-experienced person do most of the hands-on work, while the bus factor sits next to them, coaching and explaining what to do next.

Do this until the less-experienced person knows how to accomplish one task without the bus factor's help, and then either move them both to a new task, or have the newly experienced person pair with some less-experienced member of the team to achieve the same goals, only this time as the coach.

The best way to learn is to teach, and by teaching, the new person grows and learns the new task in a much deeper way than by being coached by the expert.

Bus factor as teacher

Put the bus factor in charge of a project that requires multiple people to accomplish tasks relating to the bus factor's area of knowledge. Then make sure part of that project is the bus factor teaching others how to accomplish this.

You can ask the bus factor not to work hands-on in their area of knowledge for one or two days a week, allowing others to take over. This might feel scary, but it's a great way to get the team up and running fast.

Try assigning a full-time apprentice to that expert, and make sure they pair as much as possible.

Avoid creating bus factors

You can't always prevent bus factors from sprouting, but you can minimize the likelihood of that happening in the following ways.

Pairing

The more pairing your team does, the less likely that only one person knows how something works.

1-1 code reviews

It's almost as good as pairing: each code check-in gets personally reviewed locally or via remote call (for example, Skype) with at least audio. This provides learning because it involves a conversation.

Rotation (support, scrum master, build)

Set a daily, weekly, or biweekly rotation on tasks that are bus factors, or with new tasks to prevent them from becoming bus factors.

Pushing people out of their comfort zone instead of asking the veterans to do it

If a new task comes up, select the person on your team with the least skills to accomplish it (assuming it's not high-risk). If it is high-risk, save that thought for a low-risk task (don't tell me everything is high risk!).

Next up

In the next chapter, I'll discuss survival mode, which, if you don't take care of your bus factors, you can easily fall into.

Summary

- Bus factors are among the most prominent problems that can lead an organization or team into survival mode. In the theory of constraints model, a bus factor is a constraint, a bottleneck that forces a slowdown, because it can only handle a certain amount of work at a time.

- Bus factors can cause many problems including demoralization, discouraging team growth, and becoming a single point of failure that halts productivity.

- You can mitigate bus factors by having them share as much knowledge as possible through pairing, teaching, coaching, or any means that shares what's in their heads with other people's heads.

- Detecting, avoiding, and dismantling bus factors are huge parts of being a leader who grows their team.

Part 2

Survival mode

He who is not courageous enough to take risks will accomplish nothing in life.
— Muhammad Ali

Chapter 4 deals with survival mode, the first of the three modes of operation under the elastic leadership model. Many teams are in survival mode, and the hardest thing about it is that it's usually a downward spiral—things generally tend to get worse and worse when you try to fix it. We'll discuss how you can get out of this mode and move into learning mode.

4

Dealing with survival mode

This chapter covers

- *What survival mode means*
- *How to get out of survival mode*
- *How to utilize command leadership*

*S*urvival mode (I sometimes also call it the *survival phase*), where I think most teams are located these days, is what I define as "not having enough time to learn."

Are you in survival mode?

If your team is constantly chasing its own tail and putting out fires, instead of having time to sit down and experiment, learn new things, and apply them in a manner that makes them stick, then you don't have enough time to learn.

Can you send your team to a unit-testing course for a few days? Maybe. But when they come back, how much extra time do you provide for your team to apply what they've learned at a slower pace of development (also known as *deliberate practice*)? Twenty percent more? Not nearly enough. As I'll discuss in this chapter, 20% won't begin to address the need. In fact, 200% to 300% more time is the minimum you should allow.

By not creating this extra slack time, you put your team back into survival mode. They will spiral back into old habits because of the constraints put on them.

The survival comfort zone

As chaotic as survival mode may sound, I've observed and sometimes experienced that it's quite easy to stay in this mode. In fact, as annoying as it may feel to always chase and put out fires, many people seem right at home with this stressful state of mind and are comfortable with such a role—staying up late, fixing that build, fixing that late-night bug—being a hero of sorts.

For some, being in a constant state of survival mode and fixing things that should have already been fixed is within their comfort zone. Within that zone, they know how to operate and what others expect of them, and, most importantly, they know how to succeed in this cruel world. In fact, they excel at working where others feel terror or want to quit. They excel at putting out fires. It's *what they do.*

Survival mode is a warm and fuzzy place where only those who have painfully learned how to handle things properly can tread without fear and walk between the pitfalls. Always within a hair of failure, they magically come, tired and fuzzy-eyed, out of the fog of war, saying, "It was tough, but I got it working." That warm and fuzzy feeling of knowing what should be done when the crap hits the fan serves to perpetuate survival mode.

Even more worrying: survival mode perpetuates itself. When we're in survival mode, we tend to stay there and not even attempt to get out. It's a sort of addiction cycle.

The survival mode addiction

We convince ourselves that the current course of action (putting out the fire) is the only one that can make us feel better and help us through the current situation.

For example, we're faced with a dilemma: fix a fire or refactor the code (improve the quality and maintainability of the code without changing its functionality) to prevent the fire from flaring up again. What do we do?

We convince ourselves that putting out the fire *now* will let us rest a bit in the near future, and we fix what aches the most. The *next* time this dilemma occurs, though, we remember that the last time we had this dilemma we made a choice that made us feel better immediately. We turn to that choice again.

This addiction cycle of repeating something that only drives us further into the abyss can only be broken by

- Realizing that we are in such a cycle and that we are over-committed
- Finding the courage to break the cycle by taking a risk and removing some commitments

Next, you'll see what steps you can take to get out of survival mode.

Getting out of survival mode

To get out of survival mode, you have to worry about one thing: creating *slack time* as a standard in your work process. To do that, you'll need to remove some commitments, and that's unfortunately a risk that many team leaders are afraid to take. If you also are afraid, here's something I read in Jerry Weinberg's book *Managing Teams Congruently*:

> *If done well, management is a tough job, which is why the pay is premium. However, there will always be those managers who want to get paid for the hard parts of management work without doing them.*

That's an important lesson to those of us who choose the path of leadership.

But what if you do create slack time? By creating slack time, you can start using it to practice new techniques, and, by definition, you're no longer in *survival mode,* but in *learning mode,* which is what the next chapter deals with.

How much slack time do you need?

The book *Slack: Getting Past Burnout, Busywork, and the Myth of Total Efficiency,* by Tom DeMarco (Broadway, 2001), talks about learning-time productivity being up to 10 times less than normal productivity.

If you're learning test-driven development (TDD), for example, that could mean that for a month or two, your developers might be up to 10 times slower implementing the same number of features because they need to experience writing them in an unfamiliar test-driven way. It might not be that bad for other types of learning, but you must be prepared for the many hours you will need to allocate away from other work.

If you can't accommodate for learning, perhaps you're in survival mode.

Making slack time—required actions

How do you drag your team by the hair out of survival mode to begin learning? You can start by understanding the mess you're currently in.

Find out your current commitments

Making slack time is about getting rid of some of the commitments you already have; you can fill up that time with valuable learning experiences. To know which commitments you want to let go of, you have to start by finding out what you're already committed to. One of the simplest ways to do this is by hanging up a task (dry erase) board on a wall. Put on that board three simple columns:

- A to-do column, which will contain sticky notes of tasks that await action over the next month

- An in-progress column, which will contain sticky notes with tasks currently in progress
- A done column, where sticky notes that list completed tasks will live

Also, make a special area on the board for sticky notes that you will be removing from the to-do and in-progress columns in favor of learning time.

Round up the team, and ask each person what they're currently working on, even if it's not written anywhere. Make sure to put a sticky note for that in the in-progress column. Go through the tasks for the next month with the team and make sure you didn't miss anything. When you're finished, you should have a clear (and often gloomy) picture of what's happening.

Find out your current risks

Now it's time to see what hidden things might be holding you back. One technique I recommend is called *future memory*. Assemble the team, and ask a simple question: "Imagine it's six months from now, and our project has failed completely. Why did it fail?"

If your team feels comfortable enough with you, be prepared to hear some things that might surprise you. If you don't hear anything surprising, this would be a good time to have private one-on-ones with each person on the team to see if there are things they would be more comfortable saying in private.

Make a personal list of any risks discovered and, if you uncover any in-progress tasks that people are doing that haven't yet been documented (private pet projects for the CEO, marketing requests that aren't listed anywhere, and so on), add them to the in-progress part of your wall.

Plan a red line

Now that you know your current commitments as a team, it's time to plan a *red line*. That's the point in time when you plan to schedule learning time as part of work. After the red line, you commit to make time for your team to learn.

The red line can be a month from now or at the end of the next iteration. Anything more than a month into the future increases the risk of losing focus on the current task, and interest in learning time may decline into apathy. Once you have a red line, you have a deadline. Your job is to clear enough fires before the red line, allowing you to feel comfortable scheduling learning time.

The only way you'll feel comfortable after the red line is if you remove some of your current commitments—the ones you have on the wall now. Before reaching the line, you make a dash to put out fires. Estimate how many fires you'll be able to put out before the red line arrives. For whatever fires you can't put out before then, you will have to delay your commitment to achieve them on their current schedule.

Past the line, your schedule will include tasks, but fewer than usual. How many fewer? It depends. Learning time, the time when your team experiences new skills and applies them to its current work, can slow productivity by a factor of 10. Although in theory you should allot up to 10 times more time for each task for a few months, you should realistically plan for at least 2 or 3 times more than normal.

Based on how things go, you should add more learning time by removing commitments or by adding more buffer time to the current commitments. In this case, the word *buffer* is not meant to denote the "time we might need but currently don't have." It signifies "time we need to practice new skills."

Initially, removing half of the tasks you have or allotting tasks double time might seem crazy. But imagine a team learning TDD. In fact, maybe your team tried to learn that. Written in a test-first manner, the same code can easily take three to five times longer to write than when not using TDD (this is only from my personal experience).

How do you remove commitments?

You remove commitments by informing whoever needs to know. Your boss. Your stakeholders. Everyone who should care. Here's what you do:

- Show them the list of current tasks in progress.
- Explain to them that many of the current tasks could have been avoided if the team had had enough time to learn and become more professional (give some concrete examples).
- Explain your outlook for the next few months, in terms of commitments.
- Explain the gains from this move: reinventing the team as a professional team that makes fewer mistakes and learns from the ones it makes.

Before you decide that this step isn't for you, for various reasons, here are some reasons why you should do it anyway.

Why slack?

It's easy to let this whole thing go in an effort to keep up with the daily stuff. Why would you want to tackle even more hardship than you're already tackling on a daily basis? But adding the slack will make or break your efforts. If you don't succeed in securing more slack time, you won't get more time to learn, and you won't be able to grow your team away from future survival modes and teach them the necessary skills to deal with the world.

Remember why you're doing this

You're going to go through this whole ordeal to become the team leader you wish you always were—someone who fights for the team's right to learn and to always improve. This isn't an easy task.

In fact, it's quite hard because it involves a bit of risk. Not as much risk as you think, but still, it is a risk.

The risk of losing face with upper management

You could lose face by admitting that things aren't going well. This might be a win according to some, because you'll get more respect. You can't be the only one who noticed things aren't going that great, right?

Nevertheless, it's going to feel a bit scary and risky. But remember, that's what you get paid to do: make things better, in the most professional, clear, and transparent way. Losing face is part of the game, and any would-be leader should be prepared to face such tough situations.

The risk of failing

Yes, it's possible things won't go as smoothly as you wish. It's possible you may not put out *all* the fires you promised by the red-line date. But you will learn from this experience and become better and fix things as you go (change the red line or remove more commitments).

This is what you're being paid to do

What is the job of the supervisor at a car repair shop? If you ask me, when I come to the shop, I expect the supervisor to see to it that my car is fixed relatively quickly and that it won't hurt my budget too much. But from their point of view?

The lousy ones believe they get paid to decide on the shift schedule. The good ones feel they get paid to have a great workforce that's always ready and able to service the cars in a way that makes the customers happy. They're paid to make sure everyone in the shop knows what they're doing and how to handle any car that comes in the door.

Your manager might say that you get paid to ship software—or induce your team to ship software. That means you need to do everything in your power to make your team the best at delivering that software, dealing with any needs that come up and solving problems quickly, without experiencing any bottlenecks.

Translated: You're being *paid* to make tough calls and judgments to the best of your knowledge and ability to achieve this. You're being *paid* to get your team to a level where they do things professionally. You're being *paid* to keep taking the team to the next level of performance and professionalism, because that's what will allow them to write and deliver the software.

From some perspectives, all this may seem to be undervalued, but it's what's needed to get what's requested—working software that can deliver real value over time.

But suppose management tells you, "Thanks, but no thanks. No need to grow our teams. Just write the damn thing." My initial reaction to that position is to flee that workplace and find another place where management wants people to make the best of themselves.

You don't have to leave, because this might be a good story you can keep to yourself, as you continue to work quietly at getting more slack time. A year from now, if all hope is still lost, perhaps it's time to pack up and go, but try to show results first. Create slack time with guerrilla maneuvers, and show success patterns to management when you have some numbers in your hands.

Realize that you're going to break your own patterns

Yes, I'm going to repeat myself now, only because this will happen many times. It's going to be scary and annoyingly unfamiliar. You won't be sure what to do at each specific point, and you'll sometimes have to rely on your instincts and a bit on my advice.

Getting out of your comfort zone is, by definition, uncomfortable, but that's how you learn new skills. In his book *Becoming a Technical*

Leader (Dorset, 1986), Jerry Weinberg tells the story of how he plotted his scores in the game of pinball. The score seemed to be consistently going up over time, meaning that he was becoming better, but *before* every large quick rise in points, there was a *down slope* in points. These happened when he discovered new, interesting facts about the game he was playing.

For example, he discovered that when you have more than a single ball at the same time in the game, you earn double the points for every hit. When he discovered this, he started *aiming* to have more than a single ball in the game.

When he first began doing this, he was bad at it. In fact, he was a worse player and scored *fewer* points than before using this technique. But as he got better at the approach, his total score went up higher than his usual average score.

In short, he learned how to look at and play the game differently, and to do that, he had to let go of his "sure footing" and unlearn things he had learned. To get to the next stage and to become *much* better than you are, you have to let go of the things you already know. You have to let go of the safety of the current position you're in, to allow you climb to the next level. The same applies to what you're about to do as a team leader. You're about to take a risk, do something you've never done before, and change circumstances that seem almost unchangeable. In the process, you'll learn many new things that nobody said aren't scary.

Nobody said you won't fall down a few times while you learn a new skill. Eventually, you realize that in life you always have to get uncomfortable before you learn new skills, and this is a phase of learning—you'll learn to even *like* it a bit. When this happens to me—when I feel uncomfortable, annoyed, or scared—there's also *another* voice in the back of my mind that makes me smile, telling me, "Ah, I must be learning something. Cool!" You're about to learn a lot. Hold on, and don't let go of the end goal: to always get better.

Don't fear confrontation

As you break your patterns and your team's patterns, you might get into some arguments with folks who don't like change or don't trust you. Be prepared for this to happen. Many people don't like change. It's okay to disagree, and it's more than okay to say, "Let's agree to disagree," unless it's your manager. In that case, don't be afraid to say what you believe in and what you think. It's okay if they don't accept your position, but you need to try. If you don't try, you'll never know if they might agree with you.

Don't run scenarios in your head about how a conversation with someone might go. It's usually an excuse not to have a face-to-face with that someone. Realize this, and meet with that someone in person. Be calm and rational. Make sure you can live with the decision. If you can't, you should say so.

You should strive to achieve a *real change*, not the illusion of change. If you need 100% more time and you get 20%t more time, that's something you cannot live with. You have to speak up. You have to bet the farm on this. You have to be able to say, "This is the best way I know how to run this team. Let me do my job." You should be able to say, "This is how I work. If you know someone who can do this job better and get this team to be better, you should hire them."

Eventually, know that if these things aren't accepted and you don't get anything you can live with, you should try to find a place that will respect these ideas. I believe it's okay, and even expected, to change jobs based on your work values. Don't stay where you're not appreciated and where you can't change things. Don't stay in a place that makes you feel miserable.

Commit to a place where you can live with how things are going or can change things enough that you can live with them. If you accept survival mode as a fact of life, it's your fault as much as it is everyone else's—maybe yours even more because it's *your* job to stop midway and raise the flag if something is wrong. It's your ethical responsibility.

It's your ethical responsibility *not* to tell yourself, "Well, I told them. Now it's on them," and then stay and do the same old thing. That's a cop-out. It's up to you to make something out of this role you've chosen to fulfill. Being a leader can, at the beginning, feel quite lonely, but it can also feel amazingly fulfilling to drive for a real change you believe in.

Don't despair in the face of nitpickers

You might come across some "good souls" who will, with a smile, let you know about all the different ways you could have done this and all the things you should consider before doing this. It's okay to listen, and it's okay not to accept advice. It's important that you stay focused. Your focus is to get the team out of survival mode, to make time for your team to learn new things, and to improve the team. You might need to be a bit more *command and control* in your actions.

Command-and-control leadership

When the ship is sinking, the captain doesn't call a meeting. The captain gives orders. To get out of survival mode, you need to save precious time—time you will need to put out the fires on your way to learning. During survival, your goal is also to prevent mistakes made by the team, if you can detect them, and save time by making decisions on topics that, if you have meetings about them, will take a long time to decide in a team manner.

Yes, this feels like it goes against most of the ideas of trusting your team and letting them self-organize, but it's likely that the team itself isn't ready for self-organization. Team members may lack the skill to solve their own problems when faced with issues outside their comfort zone.

One of the common symptoms betraying a lack of skills to self-organize is that the team keeps expecting the team leader to solve all of their problems. They might have learned to do that from you or from their previous team leader, but, much like an animal that has been kept in a zoo, letting them go alone into the jungle will likely get them frustrated and stuck trying to negotiate a maze of issues they're not used to dealing with. It's likely that letting them self-organize without learning the proper skills is partly the reason you're in survival mode.

Correct bad decisions

If your team decides for some reason not to use source control or use a zip file mechanism as source control, you step in and make a choice for the benefit of the team—to use proper source control tooling (for me this translates to "avoid ClearCase!").

There's no time to start debating such a decision. Now is the time to get out of survival mode. There will be plenty of time to decide and learn different configuration management options later, in the learning phase.

Play to the team's strengths

Now also is the time to get every team member to do what they do best, not to challenge them to do something they will do slowly or hate to do. If someone is a DB expert, let them handle the DB until you get out of survival mode. You don't have the precious time to let them do anything they aren't 100% productive in (unless you don't have anyone else).

Get rid of disturbances

If someone is a bad influence on the team, for example, always pessimistic, your responsibility to the team is to remove that problem.

A beta reviewer for this book asked, "It's not clear how I'd know if someone was being a 'bad' influence by resisting changes, especially if they feel they have a valid point of view. How do I decide?" If someone resists changes quietly, sitting with you, during a one-on-one conversation, they're not a bad influence. They're not influencing anyone, because you are the only two people in the room.

If someone resists changes in a room full of developers, they might still not be a *bad influence* because discussion and developers who speak up about things that bother them should be welcome in team meetings.

But having someone question decisions in the middle of survival mode in front of the whole team can be a show stopper, or at least slow down the start of the transition to learning mode. Now is not the time for too many questions. Too much doubt, particularly in difficult times, can bring down an entire team.

One way to handle dissent is to have a one-on-one talk and explain that for now, until you're out of survival mode, negative talk is unacceptable and that there will be time to talk about improving things when you have learning time available.

Another way is to move that person into a separate room for the duration of that survival phase or have them work on a different project or team for the duration of the survival phase. It may seem harsh, but harsh times sometimes call for harsh measures.

I'll add a warning here: I'd try the one-on-one first, but I wouldn't waste too much time having many such talks with the same person. The amount of time and energy you put into making this person play well on the team will be a burden—precious time and energy you'll need to get the team out of survival mode. You'll have plenty of time to work with that person on their team skills when you're in learning mode.

On a related note, there's always the noted "no downers" rule, in which you don't allow immature behavior within the team. Phrases like, "I knew it would never work," count as downers in this book.

During transformation you'll likely need to...

Once you have a green light from management to add slack time and to begin growing out of survival mode, you might need to make several changes to the way you manage yourself and your team. I'm saying "might" because you may already be doing some of those things, not because I think these changes are optional.

Start spending more time with the team

How much time? At least 50% of your time should be spent either in the team room or talking or working with one of the developers. Move your computer to the team room. Make that your base of operations. This will allow you to become a "bottleneck ninja"—you will be able to detect when someone is stuck or the team is stuck and help steer them away into more productive waters.

In survival mode, you need to make navigation corrections all the time, to make sure your vision of a learning team is realized. A stuck team cannot put out the fires and cannot move on to learning mode because they haven't made enough time for it. To clear 50% of your time, you'll need to remove yourself from meetings.

Find all the meetings where you feel you are contributing little or nothing at all and the ones where you are benefitting the least. Some regularly held meetings might only require your presence every other time, and some you can let go of completely. Cancel them as part of your overall effort to be more with your team. Use the same lines of reasoning that you used when getting rid of commitments. Your team can't function and get out of survival mode without you at the helm.

To work through the "needy" problem, you'll need to be there in case your team gets stuck; later on, when you have time to learn and teach, you can teach them to solve their own problems, and they won't need you as much. There has to be a time investment first, and it has to be you; you are the one who leads the team.

What if you're not a technical team leader? It's still vastly important that you be there, to see any team problems that come up and how your technical leader is solving them. You should be there to see if there are any people problems you can solve in some way. You should also be there for the technical lead to prevent them from getting stuck answering a question that has to do with the vision or direction the team is taking.

Be there for your team. Show that your words are not empty. Show that you are there for them as much as you expect them to be there for the company. If you ask your team to work long hours, you should be the last to leave during survival mode. If you leave before they do, you will create, at some point, a silent mutiny where people don't work but appear to. Resentment is a powerful enemy. You should be there feeling their pain while getting out of survival mode. You should be there to set a personal example. If you want to get out early, tell them they can get out early too, but don't ask them for unreasonable tasks in that time. Be there for what needs to be done and for however long it takes, until you get out of survival mode. If longer hours for are needed for a month, you should be there.

Personally, I'm against longer hours because I feel they generate tired employees who will break at crunch time or will create more fires. But I'm okay with a couple of days that are longer than usual to solve something that has gone horribly wrong, as long as it's not the norm.

Take ownership of your team

Your team may be taking tasks from multiple stakeholders. That's not a bad thing per se, but if your team is in survival mode, it might be that the team's lack of skill or technique in handling multiple stakeholder requests at the same time is one of the causes of survival mode. If a team member says "yes" to a task because they don't want to let down the requesting party, without regard for the current schedule and commitments, that's a cause for action.

One possible action could be to make the decision for the duration of the survival phase, and until otherwise stated, that you will be the only funnel through which the team will be taking tasks, and stakeholder conversations should take place through you. This can help make sure the team stays focused on fixing the current fires and also gives you the opportunity to take control when conflicting requests come in and act accordingly.

For example, you could talk to the stakeholder and explain the current priority of the tasks. You could replace a current task with a stakeholder task. As long as you're in control of what the team does, you're able to direct the team out of survival phase. If you don't control your team, someone else will and probably already is.

Learn how to say no by saying yes

One way to refuse stakeholder requests is by letting the requesting party realize for themselves that there are better ways to spend the team's time. One of the best ways I know to accomplish this is by using the task board with sticky notes of what's currently in progress and what's coming up, sorted by priority (high-priority tasks are closer to the top).

If your stakeholder wants feature X, bring them up to the wall and say, "Okay, which feature do you want to move down in order to build this?" Ask them to take down a feature from the in-progress column or the to-do column. This usually leads to an interesting conversation with the stakeholder about what each task means and how much time was estimated for it. By the end of the conversation, either the stakeholder will realize where the task fits, or you will. Either way, what wins is the value generated for the company.

Start doing daily stand-up meetings

This technique is critical to get the team in the right mindset on a daily basis. Each day, you have a team meeting lasting no longer than 10 to 15 minutes. In the meeting, each person goes through three basic questions:

- What did you do yesterday?
- What are you going to do today?
- Is there anything stopping you?

These questions are as much for the rest of the team as they are for you. Through the answers, you get to find out about team members who may be stuck working on the same task alone for more than a day or two and pair them up with someone.

You can also discover if people are working on the wrong thing or focusing their energy down a path that's not productive during the survival phase. The team gains important insight as to what's going on and what the main focus is. They don't work in their own bubble, but instead they feel more like they're part of a larger effort. Having a daily stand-up meeting (yes, you stand up during the meeting; it takes less time) helps you get rid of unnecessary, boring team meetings.

Before I get into the subject of code reviews in the next section, I want to discuss the notion of a *broken window*, because lack of code quality and broken windows go together hand in hand.

Understand the notion of broken windows

A *broken window* is a line that can be crossed. It relates to the broken windows theory, which states that if people see an opening to do something, they will take advantage of it to eventually do whatever they want. You can read more about this concept at http://en.wikipedia .org/wiki/Broken_windows_theory.

To summarize, the broken windows theory was first introduced by social scientists James Q. Wilson and George L. Kelling, in an article titled "Broken Windows" that appeared in the March 1982 edition of *The Atlantic Monthly*. The title comes from the following example:

> *Consider a building with a few broken windows. If the windows are not repaired, the tendency is for vandals to break a few more windows. Eventually, they may even break into the building, and if it's unoccupied, perhaps become squatters or light fires inside. Or consider a sidewalk. Some litter accumulates. Soon, more litter accumulates. Eventually, people even start leaving bags of trash from take-out restaurants there or even break into cars.*

How do code reviews relate to broken windows? Turns out sloppy code reviews are an entryway for broken windows. Read on.

Start doing serious code reviews

Code reviews are a great tool for teaching and learning, but during survival mode they can be used to mitigate a code-quality problem. As a team leader, if you realize there's a problem with the quality of the code that generates more fires than you're able to fix, it's time to do some serious code reviews. By serious, I mean full commitment to the task.

Here's what worked for me: *no piece of code gets checked in to source control without a code review.* Yes, even if it's one line of code. Even if it's an XML file, I still review it.

At the beginning, as a team leader, I did the code reviews. It slowed down the team, but the code quality improved. Effective code reviews are *not* done via a tool or remotely—they're done when you're sitting side by side with the person or pair who wrote the code. This personal approach allows you to share and teach much more information than you can pass with a text-based tool. Don't skimp on this! If you're going to do code reviews because your code sucks, do them right. Otherwise, if you compromise on the quality of the code review, you create a "broken window."

If you decide that "some code" doesn't need to get reviewed, that's a broken window. Eventually people will move the bar of what constitutes review-worthy code higher and higher until there's no line. By setting an "everything, no exceptions" policy, you ensure that there's no bar to move. Everything is included. During survival mode, that's important.

What if your team is larger or distributed?

What if your team is large?

If you have more than, say, seven people on your team (Google "Pizza Sized Teams"), things become less manageable. It also makes code reviews much harder. In that case, try first to break the team into smaller teams, and then teach one person on every team how to review and, more importantly, how to *teach* the other people on their team how to review code.

If you can't break up the team, assemble a group of people (about one per five people) and ask them to be the code review gate watchers, and then continuously sit with a different person of that team *while they review other people's code.* That could help you see where they can be better reviewers, coach them on missing techniques, and scale up the code review process, without sacrificing communication and shared knowledge.

What if you're part of a "wide team" —a team that's distributed?

You might not have the option of having your leader sit with you, and that's too bad. You have to use other means, like screen-sharing tools, voice software, and the like. I'll recommend a couple of tools for those situations, but know this is never going to be as good as the real thing, and you should make it your goal to have at least some scheduled times where people come in and sit down with one another.

About tooling—at the risk of dating myself as soon as the book publishes—I use a combination of TeamViewer for screen sharing and Skype for audio in the background. TeamViewer is free, and you can give the remote viewer the controls that allow them to code and change text in your local machine. This can be a bit laggy, unless your internet connection is amazing.

On Mac and Unix, and for Vim lovers (the text editor you will love to hate and hate to love), use a combination of tmux and iTerm2 with Vim over ssh, and be amazed at the world of wonder before you. For those who lived then, it feels like BBS all over again, but it works.

If you're not a technical manager, Google these terms, and get a better understanding of what you want people to use to communicate more effectively.

Next up

If you keep at it and live up to the principles outlined here, I'm sure you'll begin making time to learn. In the next chapter, I'll discuss what to do with this time and how to grow people to become self-reliant and self-organizing as a team.

Summary

- Survival mode can be defined as having no time to learn, or not using your slack time to deliberately practice new skills. Creating slack time is one of the core tactics for getting out of survival mode, but it requires taking a possible risk of losing face, or telling unhappy news to your management. But this is part of the territory and part of what real leadership means.

- Getting out of survival mode also means sometimes changing your leadership tactic to a command-and-control style. When the ship is sinking, the captain doesn't call a meeting. The captain gives orders. This is sometimes crucial because the point is to make time for learning so you won't have to use command and control anymore. You want the team to move into learning mode to self-organize, but they can't do that without practicing the skills they're missing.

Part 3

Learning mode

I hear and I forget. I see and I remember. I do and I understand.

—Confucius

Chapters 5 through 7 deal with learning mode—the second of the three modes. Chapter 5 discusses how learning happens (mostly through ravines). Chapter 6 talks about commitment language and how it helps to surface issues that people might not be comfortable talking about with you. We'll move to challenging your teams into ravines in chapter 7—a key technique for successful leaders, which can also be a double-edged sword if abused.

5

Learning to learn

This chapter covers

- *What learning mode means*
- *How to identify future pitfalls*
- *How to use trends to plot your future*

Learning mode can be defined as follows: *you have slack time and are using it to do deliberate practice of new skills.* It usually requires people to get out of their comfort zones, because acquiring new skills presents a challenge.

What is a ravine?

In his book *Becoming a Technical Leader,* Jerry Weinberg describes how he visualized his improvement at pinball. I talked briefly about this in chapter 4, but I plan to go a bit more deeply into it now to show how learning works. He plotted his points over time on a chart, as shown in figure 5.1.

At first glance, it seems there's steady progress—a steady learning curve in which he keeps getting better and better at pinball. But something interesting happens when you zoom in on the chart. It turns out the progress isn't steady at all; see figure 5.2.

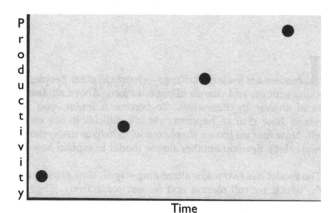

Figure 5.1   Learning rate

In this image, you can see that there are two types of "progress":

- There are *plateaus* where the learning progress is slow and steady.
- There are *peaks* in which there's a lot of quick learning.

What happened at those peaks of learning? Those were the places where he discovered something new about how to play the game—something that *changed* the game for him. In a way, it was a new paradigm about the game. For example, in one instance, he discovered that having more than a single ball at once in the game awarded double points for every hit. When he mastered the new

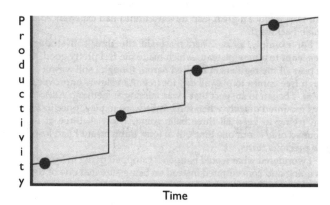

Figure 5.2   Close-up on the learning rate

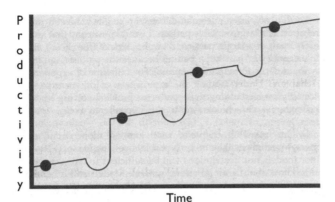

Figure 5.3   Learning rate with ravines

paradigm, he became a better player than he used to be, which accounts for the *peaking*.

As technical people, we should be used to learning new things. If you know more than a single programming language, you've already been through this peak. But there's a deeper meaning lurking in this story.

What happens when we show more points? Take a look at figure 5.3. Notice how before every peak, there's a *ravine*—a drop in points/productivity/ability before the big paradigm change. Those ravines are the adjustment phases.

> **NOTE** When you learn a new paradigm, you often have to "forget" some of the things you already know and replace them. In order to master a new skill, you have to let go of your sure footing.

When you learn a new programming language, initially you're awkward and error-prone. Sometimes you can't even write a simple "hello world" program without going through a dozen tutorials. You're far less productive when learning a new paradigm such as a programming language than when working in an area where you're already skilled.

In time, you become faster and more productive, and soon you look back and realize you're now a much better programmer than you were, because you know two different languages, and you've seen various perspectives of the same goal being achieved in different ways.

Our truest, richest learning comes from jumping into ravines, not from staying safely on a plateau. Ravines are everywhere in our lives, and they're the things that people usually refer to when they say, "What doesn't kill you makes you stronger."

Having kids is a perfect example of diving into a ravine. When my wife and I were newlyweds, we did lots of things together and were living it up. We used to travel a lot internationally and camp out twice a month. I remember complaining that there weren't enough hours in the day to do all the stuff I wanted to do. Then we had a baby.

The baby ravine

Once our first son was born, we instantly declined as human beings capable of managing ourselves, our lives, and our time. We couldn't even manage our sleep, and we became extremely tired. Close family visited us almost daily to bring us food. We were too tired to cook, and I remember random naps in various places around the house based on when the baby fell asleep.

It was both an amazing and difficult time for both of us, but a few months after our son's arrival, things started leveling out a bit. We learned to manage *his* sleep better, we learned to manage *our* sleep as a turn-based game, we started taking the baby out more, and we slowly made our way back into the normal-people territory.

A year into parenthood, we looked back at life before having a son, and we couldn't believe how much free time we had that we didn't use. We managed to accomplish the same number of things as before his birth, but now we had a full-time child. We were different people after this ravine, and we were *better* people in many ways. The challenge taught us a lot.

For a while, we were doing great. Then we had our second son. We instantly declined as human beings, unable to manage our sleep routine and struggling to take care of two kids. For example, when we had one child, we could take turns sleeping as the other parent watched him. Having two kids is a different story. Neither of us was able to stay alone with both kids at the same time because it was too demanding and we were too tired. We had to figure out how to divide baby-watching and sleep routines, we had to remember to make food for the older child, and a million other things became more complicated with raising the second one.

A few months after having the second child, things started leveling out again. We figured out routines, and we had the benefit of being less afraid and nervous for the second baby. When we were first-time parents, we were anxious about anything he got close to. With the second child, we were more relaxed, because we realized that children are resilient.

Six months after having the second baby, we looked back to the time when we had only one child, and we couldn't believe we had had such a hard time with one. Now, having a single child looked like a vacation. We were different parents than we were with one baby. The challenge helped us learn many things, and we had grown immensely in both technique and spirit from this.

Then, in 2011, we had our *third* son. We are definitely more relaxed, but I was still unprepared for how grueling things are with three kids. We are slowly learning to handle those crazy nights where we have a chain reaction of crying children, and we're managing to find one-on-one time with each kid. It's not easy, but we're happy.

I look back at having only two kids, and I can tell you this with a full heart, *having two children is a piece of cake*. I can't believe we ever moaned and groaned about raising two kids. Even more unbelievable is that we ever had trouble with *one child*. It's hard for me to process the fact that we couldn't even find, with a single child, the energy to make our own meals. We indeed are different people and parents now, but we had to jump into each ravine before we could come out of it stronger.

NOTE A beta reviewer for this book had this to say about my story: "Nitpickers may point out that as you adjust and adapt to your children, the children are also growing and adapting in ways that programming languages or tools don't when you use them, and that may have contributed to (but not been totally responsible for) your growth as a person. Nitpickers. Not me."

Embrace ravines

I think the true power of learning is realizing this simple fact: *ravines eventually end, and you emerge with new knowledge*. If you know this, you can start doing something incredible: you can begin plotting out future ravines that you might choose to fall into. You can plan your life as a series of learnings through ravines you carefully calculate to benefit yourself.

Becoming a team leader *can* be a great ravine for you, but only if you choose to jump in. Many team leaders keep the status quo and try not to touch or break anything. They never learn entirely new things. They never get an insanely better sense of the game they are currently playing; they slowly grind away, finding comfort in learning small things that make less of a difference.

How can you tell it's a ravine?

You might be facing a ravine if

- You're scared to take this step because you might lose face, dignity, money, or friends.
- You feel like this isn't something that's meant for you.
- It will *change* you, or how you perceive your world or your work or people you encounter (this is often hard to tell in advance).
- It will teach you new skills.

Taking the team out of survival mode by removing commitments may be a big ravine for many team leaders. On the other hand, you might be fooling yourself that you're in a ravine when you're not, if

- You're not afraid to try this new thing.
- You feel there's no risk in trying out something.
- You feel that this is something you've kind of done before, but differently.

For example, learning a new framework built into your favorite programming platform is not a ravine. It's fun, yes. But it's not risky, and you're not learning anything new about the game by learning a bunch of new APIs. You're optimizing things locally.

A beta reviewer argued on that point:

> *If the framework were an Inversion of Control Container (Google it) and you wanted to start using it in your product, I think that making that change could indeed be a ravine. It's scary. You may break things. You're likely to kill productivity while people are learning how to configure and use the IOC. And so on.*

I think there's some merit to that argument, but if it is a ravine, it's a small one. It doesn't even come close to the plummet of a real ravine. It's not the vision I have in mind when I talk about learning new skills and getting out of your comfort zone.

Why? First, learning and implementing a new framework in your code is a perfectly safe endeavor. With source control, there's little that can't be undone—even inflicting Inversion of Control frameworks on unsuspecting code.

Second, it's part of a developer's job to use frameworks, so it's not considered different or out of the ordinary to try a new one. Lord knows I've been through my share of people trying to use career-limiting frameworks at work, but no career has ever been limited by such a thing. Developers are resigned to having another framework to work around.

The really scary part in the IOC framework review is holding *other people* back, so it might be that the ravine one person encounters is *working with other people* or *talking with other people*. It is a ravine indeed, because it's a skill that needs to be learned and practiced. Many people do not try this communication skill when implementing many of the frameworks developers are hammered with day in and day out.

If a developer indicated to me that implementing an IOC framework was scary, I would plan a ravine for them where they *had* to talk to people. Implementing an IOC framework might be the trigger for the real thing—communicating with others. But IOC is not the point. The framework is not the point.

Another example of learning that's not frightening: if you're a .NET programmer learning a new language on your home machine late at night, you're not jumping into a ravine. Yes, it may be a valuable way to learn more things, but it's not a new coping skill.

A ravine might be joining a new team of people who *live and breathe* the new language and its associated culture, who will consider you a newbie on the team. Immersing yourself in a new work culture is a ravine. Playing it safe is not. Yes, you might have a family to think of, but you should *plan* to work in that new culture, if you can. You should not plan to do things half-heartedly.

A ravine can also be a long-term goal; I'd like to know math, because I was always afraid of it, and I know that when I conquer this fear I'll have a different view of my work world. I'll have a new skill that opens the door to new options I've always avoided. A ravine can be a short-term goal, such as confronting someone I'm afraid of talking to face to face.

The intern

A few years ago, I left a comfortable job as a CTO in a successful .NET-based company to become an intern at a small Ruby shop. Having come from a Microsoft-based background, I wanted to head into a ravine and learn, in the deepest way possible, what it means to be a Ruby developer. I wanted to know what I was missing, or find out if it was all hype. It was a great choice. Everyone used a Mac. I had never touched a Mac before. Everyone used the Vim text editor. I had only heard of Vim in my nightmares. Everyone was using Git source control. I had heard of it, but that's all.

It was a difficult few months for me. I felt like an idiot most of the time, but I learned things I never knew I didn't know, things you can learn only by being immersed in such a culture. For example, I learned how to do small code commits using Git. The culture of a small Git commit is one I could never have learned from a Microsoft-based company, because the way of work and way of thinking are different. I also learned the value of what I now lovingly call *Spartan development*—the idea that you use the lightest tools possible, you use zero to no debugger, and you trust tests to guide your way. I would never have done that learning in the evenings on my own, because I would not *think* of doing it.

As an intern, I was forced to do things that were out of my comfort zone and learn things I will take with me for all future work. *I know Vim.* Few developers can say they know it. Knowing Vim is like knowing regular expressions. You never know when you might need to use your skills, but when the time comes, you're ready.

Challenge your team into ravines

One thing I haven't mentioned yet is the concept of *homework*. I'll expand on this in chapter 7, but a brief overview of homework is required, because it's something you do in the learning phase.

Homework is normally done *at work*, but can be done at home if you'd like. I call it homework because it doesn't relate to day-to-day tasks, and it's not officially designated as part of your job. It's usually a task that you incorporate into your work, such as "try to say 'yes' at least three times a day," or "be the last one to speak in every conversation."

Giving people on your team homework is a great way to teach new skills. It's important that homework be a ravine-like task. If it's not scary or annoying to your team members, they might not learn anything new. You can only ask someone to jump into a ravine with open eyes after you've done this yourself at least once. You need to be able to feel what it's like to be aware of this learning opportunity and to get over your personal fears and feel great afterward. Only then can you lead from experience with the learning process.

You can inspire others to jump into ravines only when you have your own story to share about deep learning you've done and how it scared you. *Don't make one up.* If you want to learn something real as a team leader, learn to practice what you preach. Don't fake it—others will know, like you've always been able to tell when someone was deceiving you. If you don't have a story, do something real, and only then share it.

You should explain this homework concept to your team. Usually, it's better if you do it in a one-on-one meeting because some people might feel more comfortable openly talking about their reservations without others listening.

Sometimes, if the real learning is going to be a team effort (like moving the whole team to a new, more-challenging room), you should discuss the reasoning with the entire team as a group. And yes, it *will* be scary. Teaching a team how to plan and jump into ravines is a ravine in its own right. It will feel awkward and unnatural, but it's part of *your* learning.

Next up

Next, we'll discuss another important technique, commitment language, and how it can help you and your team trust each other better.

Summary

- Learning mode can be defined as using your slack time to deliberately practice new skills. Challenging the team this way can be difficult, because it requires you to push people out of their comfort zones.
- During learning mode, your leadership tactic will usually be that of a coach and mentor, with the occasional spurts of command and control, but only when the mistakes being made are too big to fix during the team's slack time. For example, "No, you can't choose not to use source control, but give me

three options for source control systems you'd like to choose from."

- True learning comes from ravines: places where things are uncomfortable and sometimes frustrating. If you sense people aren't happy, that might be a good sign that you're pushing them out of their comfort zones. Some pushback means you're hitting the edges of the box!

6

Commitment language

Specific words and phrases can be used by a team leader to discover hidden issues with accomplishing tasks and alleviate the problem of people telling you what they think you want to hear, rather than the truth.

To understand how commitment language works, we need to talk about personal integrity. When we practice personal integrity, we

1 Say we'll do it
2 Mean what we say
3 Do it (or raise a red flag)

Creating a language of commitment is about getting people to agree to something and mean it (or explain why they can't commit). The first part—agreeing to something—is part of our everyday conversation. We say we'll do stuff all the time, but often we only half-mean it, or we're unsure we can accomplish it.

Creating a language of commitment is one of the first steps toward developing team members who keep their promises. Changing the way we speak to each other is important. The language we use every day is ambiguous enough that we can feel like we said the right thing, while still feeling uncommitted to it.

What does noncommittal sound like?

Have you noticed the way you make promises? Look for words that leave room to *not accomplish* something:

- "I hope to finish it this week."
- "Let's set up a meeting."
- "I'll fix these five bugs as soon as possible."
- "We should take care of that."
- "I need to lose weight."
- "I think I can do this today."
- "I'll try to do that as soon as possible."

A way out

Notice how all the noncommittal sentences offer you a way out. If you end up failing to accomplish the thing you promised, you can always reason, "Well, I didn't say it would absolutely be done. I said it *might* be done."

Sometimes, you have good reason not to fully commit to doing something, for example, if it's not totally your responsibility. The problem is that instead of telling someone, "I can't commit to that," you end up telling them what they want to hear.

Wishful speaking

This problem of *hiding* important information is prevalent in our industry because we technical folk like to believe in miracles. We also don't like confrontation. Telling someone what they *don't* want to hear is a form of confrontation. Why squirm if we can go about our happy lives, and things will somehow work themselves out even if we don't finish what we promised? Heck, things are moving quickly, so it's possible no one will even remember what we promised to do.

And so this culture of wishful speaking prevails and spreads. People learn from each other how to make half-promises instead of real commitments.

What does commitment sound like?

I'll clarify the difference between language that indicates true commitment and language that is noncommittal. True commitment sounds like someone *stating a fact* about doing a specific thing, by a specific time or date. Here's the key sentence: I will [perform a certain action] by [a certain date].

The two basic building blocks of a sentence that declares commitment are as follows:

- You say that you *will* do something (not *might, should, want,* or any other inconclusive words). The word *will* states a fact.
- You give an expected end time or date. Without this part, the commitment is open to interpretation and is virtually meaningless. It has a big loophole: "I didn't say I'd do it *this week,* did I?"

Here are some examples of the previous sentences stated as commitments:

- "I *will* finish this *by* the end of this week."
- "I *will* send out a meeting invitation *today.*"
- "I *will* fix these five bugs *by* the end of the week."
- "I *will* take care of that *by* Tuesday."
- "I *will* lose 1 kilo *by* the end of this month."
- "I *will* do this today."
- "I'll *get that done by* 18:00."

These sentences give you no way out. They make you sign a verbal contract with the listener, a contract that you'll feel at least mildly uncomfortable breaking. This uncomfortable feeling is the beginning of integrity, and it's also a good way to surface hidden issues.

Is it under your control?

By now, you may have strongly disagreed with one of the commitments I wrote in the previous section. If you haven't, take another look at the commitment sentences. Is any one of them specifically bothering you? One of them should stand out like a sore thumb; it does to me.

If someone ever asked me to commit to something like fixing five bugs by the end of the week, I'd say, "I can't commit to that." Why? Because I can't promise to fix a specific set of bugs by a specific date. Bugs often aren't as innocent and easy to fix as they may seem; my commitment can easily be broken.

I call this kind of commitment "committing to something that's not fully under your control," and it's the subject of the next section.

Commit to things under your control

If a leader expected their team to commit to fixing five bugs by the end of the week, they'd have a problem on their hands. How might someone react under such pressure? Because the team members don't want to feel bad for breaking a promise, they'll do one of the following:

1 They'll *buffer* and commit to fixing those bugs by a later deadline.
2 They'll say the commitment words but won't mean them.
3 They'll say they can't commit to that expectation.

With responses #1 and #2, people don't mean what they say. With #1, it's entirely possible they still might not fix those bugs by the later deadline. We all know some bugs take longer to fix, because software is such a complex beast. With #2, they're telling people what they want to hear, and they're thinking, "I'll play this silly commitment language game, but I know it will never work."

In responses #1 and #2, people aren't displaying full integrity, because they're being asked to commit to things that aren't fully under their control. For commitment language to work, for *integrity* to exist, you have to *insist* that people commit only to things under their own control.

Let's see the difference.

Turn an impossible commitment into a possible one

If a team member commits to fixing bugs in a specific amount of time, as a team leader I'll ask them to change their commitment to something they can live up to, something under their control.

What's under their control? Usually, their time and what they choose to work on are the only things under their administrative control. It's important to notice when someone commits to something outside their control, and then ask them to instead commit to *one or more steps* that can lead to this desired goal.

For example,

I will fix these bugs over the next week.

should become this:

I will work at least 5 hours each day for the next week to fix these bugs.

Here's an example of a commitment that involves another person. That person is not under the team member's control; it's impossible to commit to:

I will meet with David today, and together we'll decide how to solve this.

This should become the following:

I will send out a meeting request to David today about solving this.

People feel comfortable committing to things under their full control.

What about the third response I mentioned (saying you can't commit to something)? When people have practiced integrity (discussed in the beginning of this chapter), they'll feel comfortable saying when they cannot commit, and then you'll have an opportunity to discover possible roadblocks that have never been mentioned before.

For example:

- "I can't commit to that because the CEO asked me to do another project, and I won't have time."
- "I can't commit to that because my machine isn't strong enough to crunch those numbers."

When you discover these roadblocks, you (or, better yet, your team members) can do something about them. For example, you can teach your team members how to solve these problems the next time they happen, and they won't need you to steer them in the right direction.

How do you get them on board?

It's important to realize that it's not a "me" and "them" thing. It's a team issue, and you need to be part of the team. You need to learn to use commitment language as well.

Here are the steps you can take to encourage the language of commitment:

- Assemble the team, teach them the language, and explain the benefits.
- Begin using this language in your meetings.
- Fix just-in-time language errors.

Let's discuss each of these initiatives.

Launch a commitment language initiative at a team meeting

Assemble the team in a single room, where possible, and explain the following concepts.

Now that everyone has the time to start learning new things, you'd like the team to adopt a different mindset about promises and commitments. Going forward, you'll ask people to use concrete commitment language when promising to do something. You'll be a bit of a pain in the neck over the next few weeks as you all adjust to this new way of speaking. Ask that people help each other out using the new language.

Teach the basics of the language (what words are noncommittal, what a true commitment sounds like), and demonstrate with promises people have recently made. If a pair promised the previous day to sit on something together, ask them to use commitment language to state the same promise in the form of a commitment.

Measure by feeling

Notice how using this new language affects how people make promises. Does it take them longer to decide if they can do something? Do they think twice before saying they'll do something? Do they dig deeper to understand what's required?

How often do you personally get it wrong? Do people correct your language when you get it wrong, or do you have to catch it yourself? You have to set a good example here. The more people hear you using this language, the more they'll feel comfortable using it with each other.

It *will* feel awkward at first. It *should* because when you learn new things and get out of your comfort zone, you feel uncomfortable. That means you're learning something new.

Fix just-in-time errors

Remember to help everyone on the team fix their language, as it happens, when it happens. The more you do it, the faster everyone will get used to it:

- "Would you mind using 'I will…by' instead?" (and smile!)
- "So you will…" (and smile)
- "Great, you forgot to use commitment language. Can you try?" (and smile)

But don't smile too much, I've been told; that will come off as creepy.

Don't worry about feeling like a jerk, but be nice and polite. Leadership can sometimes feel pretty lonely, even if you're not being a jerk. Take comfort in knowing you're driving your team toward higher integrity, and it takes a month or two to see a big difference.

What if they fail to meet their commitments?

If I set a meeting with you in a place downtown at 9 a.m., and on the way I realize I won't make it in time because of a traffic jam, I make sure to notify you as early as possible that I might be late. If I wait until the last minute, that's bad manners. For a project, waiting until the last minute to say something can be destructive.

What happens when people realize they can't live up to their commitments? It has everything to do with *integrity*. The basic idea is that they raise a red flag as quickly as possible.

Ask that your team raise a flag as soon as someone realizes they won't make their commitment, to the entire team or to you (if it was a personal commitment). The quicker they raise the flag, the greater the chances the team, as a team, can help out and increase the odds of that person living up to their commitment.

Finishing the commitment conversation

When someone has made a commitment to you, and it's not clear, it's useful to repeat what you *think* that person has committed to:

> *So, you can commit to working on this five hours, each day, for the next week?*

If the person says "yes," say, "thank you," and finish the current conversation. If the person corrects you, you've clarified that they did or did not make a commitment.

Always finish up with a thank-you because, from my experience, people don't know how to end these conversations. A nice thank-you helps a lot to put a "dot" at the end of this conversation.

Can commitments drag on forever?

"My project manager won't like me not committing to a deadline for when the bug is fixed, and committing to working on it a certain amount of time instead. She'll think I'm just buffering."

I've heard this concern. I find that, with some patience, it's easy to explain why some tasks can't be proven to end by a specific time. Instead you can "cap" the maximum time you can "burn" on a specific commitment, and then regroup, replan, and recommit based on what you found. This is true agility.

Look for "by," not "at"

One common gotcha team leaders often make about commitment language is asking people to commit to a specific time when something will take place. It's much better, safer, and more reassuring to ask people for an *end time:* when something will be done *by*.

Here's a bad version:

> *I'll do this at 14:00 today.*

Here are better versions:

- "I'll do this by the end of the day."
- "I'll do this by 15:00 today."

The difference is that you're not breaking your commitment if you do that something earlier than when you promised. It also gives you some leeway as to when to accomplish the thing you promised.

Using "by" instead of "at" isn't always perfect. When stating a specific time makes more sense, use a specific time, but that should, in my experience, happen rarely. Your first instinct should be to think, "Can we use 'by' here?"

Where to use this language

Use commitment language in daily stand-up meetings, in one-on-one meetings, and everywhere promises are made. Once you try this, you'll start noticing how much noncommittal language is spoken around you, among everyone you know and love.

This new skill, a better understanding of the *conversational signs* people give when reluctant to commit to something, will bring you both pleasure and pain. The pain will happen mostly when you need something from people and they use noncommittal language, but you're not in a position to get them to change that, and you need the most from them.

Take comfort that when that happens, you'll have uncovered a hidden obstruction to achieving your goals, possibly much sooner than you normally would have. That gives you more options in choosing what to do and where to save time, by not wasting resources on lack of commitment.

Next up

Now that your team knows commitment language, you can begin challenging them to learn new skills and ask them to commit to trying out different feats under their control.

In the next few chapters, we'll talk about growing people by challenging them, and about integrity and how to use integrity meetings to measure the success of your team's self-organization efforts.

Summary

- Commitment language helps you find out if there's something preventing people from achieving goals, but they don't feel comfortable telling you.
- Commitment language is also a way to get people to feel more committed when they say they'll do something.
- It's important to make sure people only commit to things they can control, or the technique can backfire when people commit to things they can't accomplish without commitment from other people as well.

7

Growing people

This chapter covers

- *Using challenges to develop a successful core team*
- *How to use "homework"*
- *Identifying potential in people*

In the previous chapter, you learned about using commitment language. It's time to use it to grow the people in your team.

For your team to be able to self-organize without depending on you, they need to learn how to solve their own problems. One of the simplest ways to encourage that is to stop solving all their problems for them; ask them to start solving them on their own. This is called *delegation*, and it may feel awkward at first, but it's part of the idea of getting out of your comfort zone and learning new skills.

You too will have to learn a new skill here: stop solving everyone's problems, and begin mentoring and challenging them to solve problems themselves.

Problem challenging

Sooner or later a team member will come to you with a "wishful problem" such as one of these:

- "We need faster computers."
- "I wish we had better communication with the customer."
- "We need to learn TDD."

When that happens, ask the wishful questioner one simple question:

What are you going to do about it?

Each word here is carefully selected:

What are you going to do about it?

This simple question, stated exactly like this, asks the person to answer using commitment language. Each word is carefully chosen to remove doubt that you're looking for anything other than commitment.

Suppose you ask another way:

- "What do you think you *should* do about it?"
- "What *can* you do about it?"
- "How do you *intend* to solve it?"

All these questions evoke answers that have loopholes:

- "I should do X." (Instead of "I will.")
- "I can do X."
- "I could do X."

As the person answers you, challenge them to use *commitment language*, as you saw in the previous chapter.

People may not get what you're asking them to say. They might keep answering in the same old ways. Remind them gently:

So you will... ?

This is not simple delegation, though. It's about teaching people to solve their own problems; it's a challenge to take action. That's why I call this *problem challenging*.

How did I react the first time I was challenged?

I remember when my leader first asked me, "What are you going to do about it?" I experienced a combination of thoughts and feelings:

- I felt angry because he asked me to do something that wasn't my job.
- I felt angry that he seemed to be avoiding work, asking others to do it instead of doing what he was paid to do (to help me!).
- I felt betrayed a bit, because I came for help and found myself staring in the mirror instead.

Some of this bad vibe happened because nobody prepared me for what was about to come. The conversation went like this.

I answered, "Well, I just came to you, didn't I? So that's what I'm doing about it." I felt good about telling him off.

He answered, "I want you to learn to do this on your own. It's a skill that you need to have if you're ever going to be a leader yourself."

That was a good answer. But who had time? I said, "I don't have time to do this (whatever it was—I don't remember). Can you give me more time?"

"Yes."

I got more time, and later I was asked to use "I will... by..." when committing to this new task.

It took me a couple of months, and some new skills, to realize that this was a great gift, instead of a horse with no teeth. Don't expect it to be easy to have this conversation with your people.

When to use problem challenging

This technique comes in handy in several places:

- Day-to-day growth opportunities
- Daily stand-up meetings
- One-on-one meetings

Let's look at each one.

Day-to-day growth opportunities

If someone comes to you with a problem, you can ask them, "What are you going to do about it?" You can mentor them and give them ideas about how to solve their problems, but first see if they can come up with ideas of their own. Challenge them to solve it on their own, with you as their mentor, but without you doing the work for them.

Daily stand-up meetings

When someone brings up a problem or hindrance in the daily stand-up meeting, challenge them and ask them, "What are you going to about it?" to see where it leads. Help them figure out the problem, and don't solve it for them. Teach them to solve the problem on their own. Most importantly, teach them the thought process that leads to the solution.

One-on-one meetings

When a team member raises an issue during a one-on-one, see if you can help them solve it on their own. Help them figure it out, and mentor them to completion.

Next, let's talk about what happens when someone doesn't live up to their commitments.

Don't punish for lack of trying or lack of success

When people are challenged to solve their own problems, it's important not to punish those who are unable to solve them. It's *their* problem, and they will continue to suffer for it. The consequence is that they will keep having the problem. If they care about it enough, they'll keep trying.

If you're not giving them problem-solving tools, though, that's an even bigger problem. You can't ask them to solve a problem and not support them when they attempt to do so.

Having their back can mean many things. Here are the two most important:

- Give them enough time to work on the problem.
- Give them permission to approach other people they need help from.

Next, we'll take a look at a simple concept I've used successfully many times, which I call *homework*.

Homework

Challenging for growth is only one of the techniques to use when people approach you. You can add a more structured and planned growth trail for team members by having biweekly one-on-one meetings where you can discuss the idea of *homework*.

Homework involves things a team member could do better, or things they *need* to improve on because they hurt the team. It doesn't have to happen outside of work, but it may not be related to the current work that person is doing (*sidework* might be a less-confusing name for some).

Things to consider as areas of growth for homework are these:

- Something they feel will inspire them
- Something that will get them out of their comfort zone (you can see they're afraid of doing it)
- Something that needs to change because it hurts the team (morale, productivity, teamwork)

Things that *don't* fit the description of homework, but seem like they do, are these:

- Learning the latest buzzword technology on the same platform (I know technology X but want to learn this framework)
- Learning a new platform without learning its culture (I want to learn Ruby, but I won't assimilate with an experienced Ruby team)

You can usually tell the difference between a true growth opportunity and a fake one if you know what to look for:

- *Absence of fear*—If the team member isn't even a little afraid of taking a step, it's probably not taking them out of their comfort zone. A good example of a true growth opportunity is switching to a different team or speaking to someone they're afraid to speak with.
- *Absence of annoyance/frustration initially*—If the team member isn't even a little frustrated or annoyed about how it's not their job to do X, you might not be truly teaching them something new. A good example of a true growth opportunity is doing work that was never part of their job description or sitting in a room with people they never had to work with.

In essence, homework is about learning a new *skill*, not a new technology. So always ask yourself and your team, "What skills are missing?"

Homework is a personal commitment, not a task

During one-on-ones, if someone takes on homework, they should treat it as a personal growth challenge, not as a work task. They shouldn't be punished if they don't do it, because they only hurt themselves. The desire to improve and exceed your own limits is what drives this homework, not a manager telling someone what to do. That's why taking on a personal homework task should be said in commitment language, but should be judged only at the personal growth and mentorship level, not at the work level.

Homework has follow-up

I consider it homework if I can get an email from a person at the end of each day or each week or have a one-on-one meeting each week about the progress they make. Any longer period of time, and we start to lose focus and lose track of accomplishment.

Homework examples

Let's say one of your team members is a slow typist. In fact, they use the mouse for almost everything. This is hurting your team—people hesitate to pair with them because of how slowly work gets done.

You can sit down with this person and ask them to consider ways to make improvement. Most devs would be thrilled to increase their typing speed. You can suggest ideas or, better yet, ask them for ideas on how to improve their typing speed. For example, get a "blind typing" teaching program and measure words per minute over a few weeks.

Another example would be someone who's always negative—you know, the "it's never going to work" type you've had on the team for a while now. The first step is to have a one-on-one with the person and explain that they can benefit much from choosing their battles. Homework for them could be to say the word "no" no more than three times a day.

Then you can ask the team member to email you at the end of each day and review when they said "yes" or "no" and why. This isn't about punishment; it's about being there as a mentor and personal reminder, someone to bounce ideas off and to give advice when needed.

It can take months for homework to change behavior or help someone craft new skills; plan on at least three to six months. Remember, one of the reasons you got out of chaos is to create extra time for people in your team to learn and experiment with new skills. Use that time, and let people use it to try these new commitments. It's important not to overdo it, though, as you'll see next.

Pace yourself and your team

It's important not to push this too far. If your answer to every question is, "What are you going to do about it?" at some point you're going to stop getting questions. It's going to be too quiet, and not because people know how to solve their own problems.

You'll see they can't, but they won't ask for help anymore. That's how you'll know you've gone too far with challenging them. Make sure to challenge people on no more than a couple of fronts at the same time. Don't *swamp* people with challenges. Give them time to work on one or two challenges at a time and then move on to the next challenge.

Now that we're pacing ourselves, let's talk about when to step in even though people are learning.

Do you have enough learning time to make this mistake?

Sometimes you'll see people going down the wrong path on a problem, and you'll have to make the decision whether you should let them follow that path and learn for themselves why it's a mistake or prevent them from making it.

That depends on how much time you can spare. If getting out of the hole they're digging will take longer than the buffer you've allowed for, you might want to take charge and redirect their efforts.

For example, suppose someone wants to do without source control. If they lose all of their work, it would take too much time to restore. Usually you can't afford that decision.

That's why, even in the learning phase when you're striving to be a mentor, sometimes you'll have to be a dictator.

Are there situations where you shouldn't grow people?

What if you have a short-term consultant on your team? What if you're the team lead for this project, no other, and there will be a new team lead on the next project? Should you work on growing people even in those situations? My answer is an unequivocal "yes."

People who come across my path, even for a short time, will get the same amount of respect, expectations, and challenge from me as if they had been there forever. I try to always leave those whom I've led better off than they were, in terms of new skills and challenges. It's an expression of my personal integrity.

If you conduct yourself this way, you'll find that people will want to work with you and will remember you even years later, no matter how short the project was.

You never know when you're going to meet those people again, and you may find hidden treasures along your future path because a few years back you did the right thing with people who didn't expect it of you. Show by example that even in the short term, you don't give up on quality (of people or of leadership).

Next up

If all goes well, people should be making progress with new skills every week. You can ask yourself, on a weekly or daily basis, "Is my team better than it was last week?"

The next step is using what you learned to get your team closer to self-organization, and measuring how close you are getting to that goal.

Summary

- Growing people can be accomplished by challenging them to get out of their comfort zone and do something that requires learning a new skill. This can be done using on-the-job techniques or with homework where people can gradually practice new skills even if they don't directly relate to on-the-job activities.

- It's important that people are challenged with one thing at a time. Too much can be overwhelming, and people will walk away from the challenges, or may choose not to involve you. It should be challenging, but reasonable, to accomplish learning the new skill, and they should be actively choosing to do this.

Part 4

Self-organization mode

We shape our buildings; thereafter, they shape us.

—Winston Churchill

Chapters 8–10 deal with self-organization mode: how to measure it and how to cultivate it using clearing meetings and influence patterns. We'll also discuss the role of the leader in this mode and how to set up special clearing meetings that help surface team issues (these aren't retrospectives, but deeper conversations).

8

Using clearing meetings to advance self-organization

This chapter covers

- *Using clearing meetings to advance team organization*
- *Identifying and utilizing team goals*
- *Structuring and examples of clearing meetings*

Self-organization can be defined as the team working independently of you, the leader, when making decisions and moving forward in a productive manner.

This chapter discusses how to use clearing meetings to advance the team gradually toward the ability and skills necessary to solve their problems without you. I've found this technique useful with my own teams.

In the previous chapters, you learned about the learning phase. In this chapter, you'll learn how to gradually move your team into self-organization while measuring your progress. To reiterate, self-organization is achieved when everyone on the team learns how to solve their own problems instead of relying on you to solve their problems for them. One crucial tool that I've found invaluable in driving the team toward a state of self-organization is *clearing meetings*.

I first learned about clearing meetings when one of my managers introduced the idea to our management team. He then implemented this as a standard weekly meeting for our team, and I've experienced this for more than two years with my own team as well as with other teams.

Clearing meetings can have several goals:

- Introduce important issues everyone should know about
- Pull the *Andon cord*, a stop-the-line trigger that makes everyone pay attention to an important issue and do something about it
- Give everyone the chance to air issues that bother them
- Gauge the current level of the team's self-organization
- Create more trust within the team
- Flex the team's self-organization muscles and remind them to solve problems on their own

It's called a *clearing meeting* because you uncover all the stuff the team knows is not working, bad feelings they've buried about the job, and information that should be shared; then you do something about it.

To understand how it works, let me describe a typical session.

The meeting

It's 9 a.m. in the meeting room. Present are Jim (team leader of team 1), Jenna (team leader of team 2), David (marketing team leader), and me.

> *Me*   "Morning everyone. As usual, we're having this clearing meeting like any other Friday. Remember, nothing is out of scope for discussion here and I expect you to speak up if you disagree with something. We're starting like any other meeting by going around the room with our usual

set of questions. Jim, is there anything you wish had gone better this week? Something you're not happy about that happened?"

Jim   "Hmm. As you know, our team was all set for a new release this week. Well, we failed to do a release even though that's something we committed to do. I know we tried our best, but something wasn't clicking. I hated how we deployed things manually instead of fixing the build script. I think that's what eventually stopped us from releasing."

Me   "OK. What are you going to do about it?"

Jim   (A little taken aback. Thinking...) "Well... hmm... I... I think we need to fix the build before doing anything else."

Me   "So you will...?"

Jim   "I will fix the build."

Me   "By...?"

Jim   "I will fix the build by this evening."

Me   "Is that really something you can commit to? Do you know exactly what's wrong with it that you're so sure it will take that long?"

Jim   "Well, I'm just guessing."

Me   "In that case, please commit to something fully under your control. For example, that you will spend X hours on it in the next couple of days until it is solved. Or something like that."

Jim   "Yeah, makes sense. I will work on fixing the build at least five hours each day of the week until it works the way it should."

Me   "Are you happy with that solution, Jim?"

Jim   "Mmhmm. Yep!"

Jenna   "Jim, if you fix the build, you're doing that thing again. That thing where you take on everything yourself because you hate wasting time explaining things to other people. That hurts my team, because whenever they need something from your team, they usually get referred to *you*, since your team doesn't know how to do anything but the simplest tasks."

Jim   "Yeah, I get it. You also said that in the last meeting. But, seriously, we don't have time for teaching everyone on my team about the build process."

Jenna   (Sighs.) You'll say the same thing in the next meeting and the one after that. Aren't we supposed to be agile?"

Me   "Sounds like survival mode to me."

Jim   (Sighs.) "I didn't realize it until I heard the words coming out of my mouth."

Me   "So what are you going to do about *that*?"

Jim   "I'll need to make more time so the team can learn about the builds."

Me   (Smiling.) "So you will...by...?"

Jim   "I will remove or change enough commitments by the end of next week, so that there's enough time for me to teach at least one person about the build. And then the week after, on Monday, I will pair on the build with Christie, I think. She always seemed interested in how the build works anyway."

Me   "OK. Are you happy with that solution?"

Jim   (Thinking...) "Yes, I think that's a step in the right direction."

Me   "OK, Thanks Jim. Jenna, anything that wasn't working for you this week?"

Jenna "Well, there was this one thing, but I'm already doing something about it."

Me "Great! If you wanna share, feel free."

Jenna "Well, not really. It was something between me and another person and we weren't getting along, but I talked with them this morning, and we're working on patching things up."

Me "Happy to hear. David, anything you'd like to share that maybe hasn't worked well for you this week?"

David "No. Nothing special."

Me "Really? Everything was just perfect? This week couldn't have gone better at work?"

David (Wrapped in thought...) "Well, you know, I think we're building the wrong product."

Jim "What do you mean?"

David "It's a long story. Let's take this offline. It's just going to make this meeting too long."

Me "No, please continue. If it bothers you, the team needs to hear this, and we might need to do something about it."

Jim "Is this about that customer-mirror test?"

(During such a test, you're behind a mirror, watching a customer use your product.)

David "Yeah. From what I saw on Tuesday, people are trying to use our product as we initially thought they might, rather than how we've designed it over the last couple of months. I have many doubts about it."

Jenna "So you're saying we should drop it all and go back to the two-month-old idea? Seriously? All that time wasted?"

David "I'm not saying..."

Jim   "David, you've only been here six months. You might be seeing things through rose-colored glasses."

David   "Well, actually, that might not be a bad thing. But before changing everything, let me show you the videos."

(David runs and gets his laptop and shows about five minutes' worth of his video highlights.)

"Now, what do you think?"

Jim   "Yeah, that was *not* good."

David   "Exactly."

Me   "OK, David, so what are you going to do about it?"

David   "Well, I want to be more sure. I want to run some more customer tests."

Me   "So you will...?"

David   "That's it, I can't do anything about that. I don't own the budget. That's you."

Me   "I have to say I'm not convinced. We might be seeing too little. We might need more tests."

David   "If you approve, I'll make calls to the company that sets these up and arrange for three more sessions by the end of today."

Me   "OK, do that."

(I write myself a note about the budget.)

"OK, David, so are you happy with this start of a solution?"

David   "Yep!"

Me   "OK then. Great. Now let's start with the second question. Jim, tell us about something good that happened for you this week or something good that was done by someone you work with."

Jim   "Well, *Blaine* is back from being sick. And he's jazzed up. Today he was teaching everyone about regular expressions. I feel like we are getting our energy back with this guy around."

Me   "Great! Jenna? One good thing?"

Jenna   "I noticed that James from my team and Joyce from David's team were working together on some numbers for the product box a couple days ago. That's the first time I saw anyone from marketing talking to anyone but me on my team. It was great!"

Me   "Cool. David?"

David   "Yeah. That was nice huh? After we talked following last week's clearing meeting, I talked to Joyce and challenged her to talk to a real dev. She said it was weird, but in a good way. In any case, my good thing is about Jim. When he spoke to that annoyed customer from Coca-Cola the other day, that really saved my neck. Thanks for taking a personal look."

Jim   "Happy to help."

Me   "OK. What's not working for me? Well, nothing. Whatever wasn't working, you're already doing something about that. So for me, everything is working great. Jim, this week you and your team tried to do a feature we thought was next to impossible. You almost made it to release, and I think next week when it *is* released, it will be amazing. Thanks. Jenna, thank you for doing such an amazing job bringing two new people into your team at such a difficult time. You're spending time with them instead of in meetings, and that's commendable. Thank you. David, you guys brought in one of the clients we lost a year ago. Great job! OK, everybody. Does everybody know what they're going to do once they leave this room?"

(Everyone nods.)

Jim   "Um... Wait. So what will I do again?"

Jenna   "You'll make time to teach your team about builds and then pair up. Next week."

Jim   "Ah, cool, Jenna. Good memory. Nice!"

(Everyone leaves.)

What just happened?

You've just read a not-so-remote account of something that happened on a real team I was on. The team had a passionate discussion about things that needed to change, and people took responsibility for their problems. The meeting ended with everyone knowing what they were going to do and feeling things were already on the way to improvement.

To understand and analyze this meeting, we have to take a step back and talk about integrity and how that fits into the picture.

What is integrity again?

I discussed the idea of integrity in chapter 6. In the example meeting, I used commitment language and made sure people exercised full integrity when making promises. When people promised something they couldn't fully control, I brought them back to reality by asking them to commit to a more realistic set of actions that would bring them to their goal. For example, when they committed to fix a bug by a specific time, I asked them to commit to working on it X number of hours each day instead.

Let's get a better handle on what happened by looking at the overall structure I used for the meeting.

The structure of the meeting

The structure follows a rather simple process and can take anywhere from 30 minutes to a few hours, depending on how burning and passionate the issues discussed are:

- "What has *not* been working for you this past week?"
- Discussion and possible detours
- "What are you going to do about it?"
- Discussion and possibly more detours
- "What *has* been working for you this past week?"
- Your closing words

Let's take a closer look.

The meeting

I started the integrity meeting by asking these three simple questions, going around the room with each one before moving to the next one.

"What has *not* been working for you this past week?"

This question is open-ended. The goal is to see if there's anything that's been missed, either at the personal or at the team level. People can get frustrated with the software world, and if you let them talk about the things that frustrate them, even if they seem small, you might be surprised at how much they're willing to share.

Things that you might look for are these:

- "The build keeps failing."
- "Documentation is lousy."
- "Team X is giving us a hard time."
- "We're doing the wrong thing."

These or other statements related to the current work environment, people, or process are valid. Looking at this question from the self-organization point of view, this question is asking, *"Is there anything that is hindering the team and needs adjustment?"*

But it's a question that the people being asked should learn to ask themselves. *You* are asking this question because it's part of the almost invisible process of training people to think about the current status quo and continuously contemplate which changes need to be done. Avoiding blind acceptance of the status quo is one of the concepts you want your team to learn.

People might at first say, "Nothing went wrong this week." Try to persist a little bit. Give examples of possible sources of concern. Try not to accept "nothing" for an answer, particularly from the first couple of people answering. Other people in the meeting will follow the lead of the first few and, if the first ones are silent, will usually shy away from saying anything.

Also note that this kind of question can raise some demons that might previously have been kept in backroom meetings. If an argument starts, try to keep it going. Embrace conflict. People who've been heard are more willing to make a commitment even if they don't like the decision made by the group or the leader.

"What are you going to do about it?"

If a person has indicated that something wasn't going well this week, ask them, "What are you going to do about it?" You may ask in a more polite manner, but remember what we talked about in chapter 6: don't use words that offer an easy way out. Here are some examples that give a way out by asking the question in a different way:

- "What *could* you do about it?" (This is merely contemplating versus requesting specific action.)
- "How *would* you fix it?" (Again, contemplating versus an actual request for action.)

Once you've challenged the person to action, make sure you get all the way to a commitment. That person needs to know what they're going to do after the meeting is over or have a timeline or end date they're expected to meet.

From the point of view of self-organization, this is an important learning tool for the person being asked. *Always* ask "What are you going to do about it?" when you hear a statement that something isn't going well. Too often, we complain about the world and don't do anything about it. Here's a situation that's much closer to us—our own work environment—and we have more say over how things work around us. We *can* influence our immediate environment, and we *should*.

For a self-organizing team, having each team member realize that they're not *stuck* in a situation, but can always *choose* to do something about it, is one of those turnaround moments. A team can begin being proactive instead of reactive. A team can begin anticipating and preventing problems, and people on the team can stop thinking they have to be miserable while doing their jobs.

You can teach your team that, as professionals, it's okay for them to feel annoyed at the way things are. They *should* be feeling happier when things are being done more professionally. Then they *should* take those gut feelings they have and apply them toward making a better work environment, product, and process.

The core lesson here again is this: don't passively accept that which bothers you. There's always *something* you can do.

The question "What are you going to do about it?"—normally asked in connection with a problem statement—contains a core lesson; you're teaching them to ask themselves this question when something bothers them.

This is the core of self-organization: when the team finds something that needs to change, they look *within* to begin solving the problem, instead of forwarding the problem to a manager.

"What *has* been working for you this past week?"

Once you've gone around the room and all the bad energy has been emptied, and you've made sure anyone who had a problem will be doing something about it, start asking this question.

There are several reasons for asking this question:

- Clear the air and give everyone a positive feeling
- Acknowledge people for their actions and efforts
- Share good news and information with the team

Try to make the answer about other people in the team or company, but don't force it. Here are some examples of answers I hear:

- "I sat with *X* from the QA department, and, for the first time, it was really helpful."
- "I pair-programmed with *X*, and we found something I was stuck on for a while. It felt good."
- "We finally released that thing we were stuck on."
- "We got new machines! Finally!"

There should *always* be something good to say. Don't let people say nothing. If they can't think of something, return to them at the end of the round. This is a lesson in noticing others and being socially aware enough to share a compliment.

Your closing words

Now that everyone has expressed what didn't work and what did work for them this week, it's your turn. You answer the first question, "What didn't work for me this week?" Now, it's possible that there was something that didn't work for you this week, and you still haven't begun doing anything about it. This is a good time to bring it up with your team and say what you're going to do about it.

For example:

> *This week I noticed that I spent way too much time on meetings instead of being there with you when you needed me. Like when the build crashed and you waited for me a whole day. So what am I going to do about it? I will block off at least 50% of my time in the coming month in the company calendar, so that I don't get this distracted again. I'll do this by the end of the day today.*

Also, as closing words, remind the team that, as an exercise, you want them to try to reach the next meeting not only with things that didn't work for them, but also with actions they've already taken. It can go something like this:

> *Next week, the day before the meeting, imagine the meeting has started and I'm asking you what didn't work well this week. Imagine your answer and my follow-up question, "What are you going to do about it?" Then, answer that question in your head, commit to an action, and then just do it. Ideally, you should come to the next meeting saying, "There was X that bothered me, but I'm already doing something about it."*

The overall point of this meeting

As discussed at the beginning of this chapter, this meeting can be used for many things. I find that it's effective for teaching a team of peers to think proactively about solving things that bother them and at the same time gauging how self-reliant they are.

At each meeting, notice how many people say, "I had a problem with X, but I'm already doing something about it." The day that everyone says that, you can say your team is self-organizing. They're proactively solving their own problems without waiting for anyone else's permission to do something about it.

Keeping the meeting on track

What happens if you notice personal attacks, stubbornness, helplessness, or other negative behavior in the meeting? If you haven't had many meetings yet, this could be the underlying team dysfunctions coming to the surface.

If this is the first time this has happened, or the first meeting, sit back and perhaps write notes about behavior you found problematic. I wouldn't necessarily do anything immediately. If a new member in the team suggests changes and gets attacked in the meeting, let them handle the fire on their own. Don't stop the meeting and take things offline. Let the team member learn how to handle themselves in a team argument. Later, after the meeting, you can sit with them in a one-on-one meeting and coach them on handling future meetings more effectively.

Conflict is not bad in such meetings. In fact, if you have no conflict, you might not be talking about the truly important subjects.

A beta reader asked if seeing negative behavior means the team isn't mature enough to have such a meeting. I think the purpose of the meeting is to take an immature team and help it grow to maturity. Delaying the meeting until you feel it's the right time will prolong the process of maturing the team.

Next up

Next, we'll talk about influence patterns and how they can aid in your quest to develop team skills in the face of naysayers.

Summary

- Clearing meetings combine commitment language, integrity values, and slack time to push the team toward learning how to solve their own problems. They're also good for measuring how the team is progressing on that path: the more issues they solve without needing to bring them up in the meeting, the more they've solved their own problems without needing your intervention!

- Clearing meetings are also a great way to find your team spirit and encourage everybody to be less political and work together, because they help to build team trust over time.

9

Influence patterns

A big part of the frustration team leaders experience is rooted in a feeling of helplessness. You believe in doing the right things, but you can't seem to get the people around you to change their behavior.

What about using my authority?

Using your authority is usually the path of last resort, unless you're in survival mode. Then, wielding authority is the *second*-best choice, after having people intrinsically motivated to change their behavior.

When you're in the learning and self-organization phases, telling people what to do is an ineffective way to teach. Helping them find their own path that results in a win for everyone is a more effective way to teach new skills.

I'll borrow some choice vocabulary from a great book called *Influencer: The Power to Change Anything*, by Kerry Patterson, Joseph Grenny, David Maxfield, Ron McMillan, and Al Switzler (McGraw-Hill, 2007).

The book details a powerful technique to help you discover what you can do to change the behavior of others.

When I teach this technique in my workshops, I remind students that the most important thing to do before they start this exercise is to find a demonstrable *physical* behavior they would like to change. Examples might include these:

- Team member X is always late to the stand-up meeting.
- X never asks for help when he's stuck on a task.
- X doesn't participate in any offer to pair-program.
- X doesn't write unit tests.

Now, here are some bad examples:

- X thinks he knows things better than everyone else. (You can't assume you know what a person thinks or feels, and this isn't a physical behavior.)
- X always argues. (Be more specific. When we meet on Y, X argues more than Z minutes.)
- X doesn't like to work on this project. (This isn't a behavior you can target for change.)

What do you do if you want to influence someone to change a *core behavior* (such as those just detailed)?

The book identifies six influence forces that are involved with change.

Category	Forces
Personal	Personal ability Personal motivation
Social	Social ability Social motivation
Environmental	Environmental ability Environmental motivation

We're likely to think of only the first two forces (personal ability and personal motivation) when we try to understand why a person isn't on board with the rest of the team. Because our profession requires us to think as logically as possible, we tend to think that if we explain a subject or a reason, then others will immediately adopt our point of view. We're stumped when that doesn't happen.

"I sent him on a two-day unit-testing course and explained all the benefits of unit testing. He's obviously lazy or doesn't care about the project."

This is what happens when we run out of options to consider: we start looking at dark crevices in our mind and putting words in people's mouths without asking for their opinion. Many times, we play this "I know what he'll say" game because we're afraid to talk face to face with that person about an issue.

This can happen subconsciously, but it's hard to deny this *does* happen to many of us. Remember, it's *your job* to do all the hard stuff, including gently confronting people and talking with them about serious issues. This has to be done in a personal setting (a one-on-one meeting), but it must be done.

Let's walk through each of the influence forces.

Force	Description
Personal ability	Do they have all the skills and knowledge to perform what is required?
Personal motivation	Do they take satisfaction from right behavior and dislike wrong behavior? Do they have the self-control to engage in the behavior when it's hardest to do?
Social ability	Do you or others provide the help, information, and resources required, particularly at critical times?

(Continued on next page)

Force	Description
Social motivation	Are the people around them actively encouraging right behavior and discouraging wrong behavior? Are you or others modeling right behavior in an effective way?
Environmental ability	Are there aspects in the environment (building, budget, and so on) that make right behavior convenient, easy, and safe? Are there enough cues and reminders to stay on course?
Environmental motivation	Are there clear and meaningful rewards (such as with pay, bonuses, or incentives) when you or others behave the right or wrong way? Do short-term rewards match the desired long-term results and behaviors you want to occur or avoid?

Now that you have the basic list of forces, let's see how you can use them in real life.

An imaginary example, using an influence force checklist

Here's an example of an imaginary checklist about someone resisting TDD (keep in mind that this differs for each person in each organization).

Force	Description
Personal ability	Yes. They took a three-day TDD course with Roy Osherove.
Personal motivation	I spoke with them, and they like doing TDD.
Social ability	No problem.
Social motivation	As much as possible.
Environmental ability	* We don't have a budget for a build machine
Environmental motivation	* When we try to spend time unit testing, our managers tell us we're wasting time. If we ship early even with low quality, we get a bonus.

I put asterisks next to the items in the right column that require work. Here I've identified two issues that need to be resolved. Solving only the build machine budget problem will not change the behavior. We have to do two things. First, we have to get a build machine. Second, we need to convince our managers to stop giving bonuses to people who ship quickly with poor quality.

For the behavior to change, you must change all the factors in play. If you change only one of them, the behavior won't change.

A note about privacy: Never discuss private matters publicly. Talk in a one-on-one setting, because it can be hurtful for people to be confronted or asked a personal question in public.

Next up

I hope this short chapter helps you figure out what underlies problem behaviors. Next, I'll present a manifesto for line managers.

Summary

- Influence patterns help you understand why you meet resistance when trying to make changes. Why is someone's behavior not changing?

- Think of it as a checklist to go through when trying to brainstorm what the possible issues might be, and as a guide on how to take action that promotes change.

- Remember that all factors need to be solved for a behavior to change. It only takes one factor to keep the old behavior, even if you've solved two others.

10

The Line Manager Manifesto

This chapter covers

- *Principles of leadership from a line manager's perspective*
- *Working with teams suffering from a lack of good leadership*
- *Working with individuals suffering from indifferent leadership*

If you're a line manager, maybe some of the things in the Team Leader Manifesto in chapter 1 didn't make sense to you. You don't exactly have a "team." Your team might be spread out, providing services to multiple unrelated projects (particularly in a matrix organization, where your direct lead isn't your hiring manager) or even multiple customers (if your employees are consultants).

Does that mean that now all you get to do is "push paper" and sign budgets? When I became a director I hoped not, but in the beginning that's exactly what happened.

In a large organization, you may feel torn away from doing "real" things that matter to people. Instead, you're thrown into a mountain of paperwork, SAP software, and other hazardous materials that'll make you twitch in disgust for hours as they suck your life away.

You feel compelled *away* from doing what's best for your team and *toward* doing what's best for the company's procedure police (to your dismay, you see how money is wasted on meaningless labor that brings nothing to the bottom line but lower numbers).

No, that's not what line managers were meant to do.

Your work as a line manager can be good for the company's bottom line, and good for your general state of mind, as long as you set goals that aren't specifically software- or budget-oriented, but instead are people-oriented.

I think the best line managers are engaged in what their employees are doing, even if they aren't in close physical proximity, and they can help by being coaches as much as being direct technical leads. It requires a bit of a mindset readjustment.

Following is an adjusted version of the Team Leader Manifesto for line managers.

The Line Manager Manifesto

For us as line managers, the goal and the way we measure our success is the overall long-term growth in skills of self-organization and self-sufficiency in each employee under our management. The rest is paperwork.

To that end:

- We accept that what each employee needs from us changes continuously based on the team they're currently in, the current project they're serving, and the current tech lead they might have. Those circumstances, coupled with the employee's skills for handling the current reality of work, mean that we, as managers, embrace a continuously changing leadership style for each employee, rather than a one-style-fits-all-employees approach.

- We believe in challenging ourselves and our employees to always improve; therefore:
  - We coach our employees to think about and help create slack time to allow them to learn by gradual practice.
  - We embrace taking risks over staying safe and coach our employees to do the same.
  - We provide "air cover" when appropriate to create an environment where they can learn and experiment without fear.
  - We circulate our employees throughout varying types of tasks as much as possible, to assist them in learning skills from across the entire organization (instead of keeping them in their comfort zone in the same project or task for years).
- We believe our core practice is leading people, not wielding machines, therefore:
  - We embrace spending at least 50% of our time communicating with our employees, face to face or as close to that as possible.
  - We embrace treating software problems as people problems, and this is what we coach our employees and leads to consider when they're stuck. It's also what we discuss with our managers when things get out of control and there's panic in the air.
  - We learn people skills and communication techniques in order to manage up and down, and make sure our employees do the same.

Survival mode

Let's consider how the Line Manager Manifesto applies to projects, teams, and individuals in survival mode.

Projects in survival mode

A project that involves a couple of your employees could be in survival mode, while another project with other employees you manage could be self-organizing.

At the project level, there's little you can do because you usually don't control the project as a whole. Team leads at the project level will have more influence changing behaviors, cultures, and practices; they should mold their leadership style accordingly based on the current mode they find their own teams in, and within the project's context.

But, as a higher-level manager, you usually have more access to the higher-level project leadership, which means you can help elaborate and influence what messages and forces act on the project.

For example, if you know that teams are measured on a metric that encourages "bad behavior" (such as measuring lines of code produced per day), you can talk to the project leadership during a meeting and explain why that metric should be abolished in favor of something that encourages better quality, maintainability, or whatever currently ails the project.

Teams in survival mode

You sometimes don't control a team either, although often line managers are also responsible for a specific team or group with some specific function in a project. If you *do* control a team, you can read this book mostly from the standpoint of a team lead. If you *don't*, read on.

Teams within projects can have their own mode of operation that's disconnected from the project's state. Ultimately this is an anti-pattern, as teams should be operating with a view to the entire project, not solely based on what's going on within the team; but that's a separate discussion.

From a line manager's point of view, there's little you can do to control a team's behavior, because that type of work is designated for team leads. But you *can* offer advice and assistance to team leads, or alert them to specific things that might be hard to see from within the team's structure. For example, a team can be in survival mode if multiple projects or managers demand things from the team at the same time, and the team becomes overcommitted.

Sometimes a friendly word with a team leader you have a rapport with can be enough to start discussing "what can we do about this," which might lead to a collaboration—they on their team's side and you on the leadership side—to bring an end to a particularly bad situation at work.

Individuals in survival mode

The individuals you manage could be in their own private mode. Some of your employees could be in survival mode that's unrelated to their current assigned project or team. For example, maybe they're new to the company and are still struggling with performing simple duties such as time management, travel expenses, and so on, and need help figuring things out. That's simple.

A more serious problem happens when individuals you manage are in a team where the team lead doesn't stay tuned to the team modes. Your employees might need the team lead to coach them, challenge them, or provide command-and-control prescriptions on what to do next.

That, sadly, happens often. If the team lead doesn't help the team grow, line managers should be there for their employees—to encourage growth, provide challenge, and give guidance when they're lost, even in the context of a specific project, team issues, or otherwise.

I believe line managers are the last line of defense against individuals being left in a vacuum by their current team or project leadership.

They shouldn't have to fend for themselves; the line manager can and should step in.

Providing help as a line manager or director can be more difficult than as a team lead, because you might not know what's going on in a specific project or team if you work in a matrix-style organization. Frequent one-on-ones with your employees are the key to discovering what personal or team mode they're in, and helping them grow to become self-organizing.

A team leader who's out of touch with the team is an anti-pattern I've seen in many matrix-style organizations, where the people who control your schedule aren't the people who control your paycheck or can hire and fire you. It's not the anti-pattern itself but a systematic environment force that can lead to the following behavior: between a line manager who feels that it's the team lead's job to take care of the people in their team, and the team lead's perception that any major issues should be handled by the line manager, *nobody* takes responsibility and rescues an employee who doesn't know what they should do next, feels overwhelmed with the amount of work, or doesn't know how to build quality into their tasks.

If the team lead neglects this duty, the line manager has to catch it, and vice versa. Many line managers believe it's fully the team lead's job to take care of such "growth" matters, or that they as line managers aren't expected to.

Sharing responsibilities is caring: team leads and managers

Everyone thinks they're right, and at the same time everyone should take responsibility. I heard someone refer to this as "200% responsibility."

This question arises: if both the team lead and the line manager take the same responsibility—to grow the individuals on their team and the team as a whole—won't *everyone* be stepping on everyone else's toes? The way to avoid that is to split the workload:

- Team leads can grow their teams in matters related to technical, team, or project matters.
- Line managers can grow their employees in matters related to everything else, such as personal growth in the company, working on multiple diverse projects to increase total skills from a company standpoint, and so on.

Learning mode

Next, how does the Line Manager Manifesto apply to projects, teams, and individuals in learning mode?

Projects in learning mode

Your employees could be involved in a project that's in learning mode. This is a great opportunity for them to learn, grow, and make progress. There should be nothing for you to do other than sit back, listen, and watch as they learn and master new skills.

Sometimes a project will be in flux, barely out of survival mode but not quite in learning mode. Team managers have gained more slack time, but they aren't using it for learning new skills. This could be another case for you as a manger to fill the vacuum that team leads may not wish or know how to do, and put your people into challenging situations that deal with something related to their project.

You can also use your greater leverage powers as a manager to talk to your fellow managers who are involved with the project and discuss the idea of growing the project teams' skills. Who knows, maybe you're not the only one in that room who has read this book!

Teams in learning mode

The situation for a team is much the same as for a project.

Individuals in learning mode

Again, share the responsibility of building skills with team leads, which allows you to focus on skills that are higher-level and might benefit many projects or teams, while the team lead might choose to focus on skills the team needs at this moment.

It's important not to burden the individual with too many challenges at the same time! One challenge at a time is usually more than enough. In fact, if you pile on two or three challenges at the same time for a person, you might build a wall too tall to climb, and that person might leave thinking you have something against them personally; *coordination* is the key here.

Self-organization mode

Finally, what about line managers and projects, teams, and individuals in self-organization mode?

Self-organizing projects and teams

You shouldn't interfere, because everything seems to be going pretty well!

Self-organizing individuals

Make sure to take on the role of a coach/facilitator, and ask the person where they want to go next in terms of their career and skills path. Only if you feel they've turned back into learning or survival mode does it make sense to become a coach/dictator and "tell" them what to do.

Other burning questions

- Are managers leaders? I'm a manager; is it possible my tech lead should be reading this book, not me?

  Answer: Yes, managers are (or should be) leaders. They surely have the potential to be, but many don't take it, and the organization suffers for it. Yes, you should read this book.

- There are some things I can't delegate or challenge other people to do (signing off on purchase orders, budget requests, time reporting sign-off, signing off on cost-center-related work, and so on). I can't grow folks to do my job, can I?

Answer: There's a great deal you can do. You can't get them to sign things, but you can instead

- Have them be there when you're going over things like budgets or important decisions to create understanding of the thinking process.

- Have them join important (and mundane) meetings you attend as a fly on the wall or apprentice, to understand how the sausage gets made and start working on their organizational (a.k.a. *political*) muscles, meeting more people and seeing what life is like outside their own work category.

Do you get the idea? If they can't do it, they can at least see *you* do it and study it up close.

Here's the awful truth I found when I got into director-level jobs: if you're a director, it's likely you've noticed that things are chaotic, to say the least, and everyone around you seems to be winging it as much as you, while keeping a straight face to appear that they know what they're doing.

You're better off trying a new way you believe will work instead of mindlessly following the crowd. If the crowd were headed in the right direction, then any current negative situation could've been avoided completely. At the very least, show initiative to try new things. High-level managers *secretly yearn* for the mid-level manager who will get them out of the current messes they're in charge of, while they take credit. This is your chance to do something that might make a dent in corporate culture and help team leads and individuals make the most of their time in your company, therefore delivering more and better value.

Next up

The remainder of this book presents notes written by other leaders, like you, and by some consultants I trust. I hope the overview of elastic leadership principles, the three team phases, and leadership styles and techniques will be helpful for you down the road. Enjoy the notes!

Summary

- Line managers can follow an adjusted version of the Team Leader Manifesto, focusing on engaging with their employees and influencing management and leaders.

- Projects and teams in survival mode that are lacking adequate team leadership can benefit greatly from the attention of proactive line managers.

- Individuals in survival mode who are lacking adequate team leadership need rescuing by a line manager who's willing to accept responsibility for encouraging their growth and development.

- Projects, teams, and individuals in learning mode can benefit from cooperation between the team lead and the line manager.

Part 5

Notes to a
software team leader

To improve is to change; to be perfect is to change often.

—Winston Churchill

Chapters 11–32 present an assortment of notes by people I asked to contribute, each with a closing note from me exploring how it ties in to the manifesto in chapter 1.

Feeding back

by Kevlin Henney

A slim figure takes to the stage, dressed in orange and black, wreathed in a bandana, his guitar flipped over and strung for left-handed play. It's the close of over three days of hedonistic and culturally shifting psychedelia and sound. Humans have recently, and for the first time, set foot in another world.

It's 1969. It's Woodstock. It's Jimi Hendrix. During his set he splices metallic whale song into his fluid solos, coaxing sounds from his Stratocaster that guitars have no business making.

This is feedback. Not the negative feedback that dampens sound and enthusiasm. Positive feedback. Not gushing and uncontrolled, neither excessive nor insincere. There is an art to feedback.

Feedback, particularly positive feedback, is normally a sound engineer's nightmare. A skilled guitarist can make it part of the performance, part of the music. For software engineers, offering and taking feedback, positive or negative, can be as much of an art form. When there's a problem, it's too easy to resort to silence or complaint. When there isn't a problem, it's too easy to resort to silence.

When you ride a bicycle, feedback is essential. Sight, hearing, and proprioception allow you to navigate and balance, to respond to the bike and the road. You respond when the bike is balanced and on a steady course: you respond by continuing to do what you are doing, preserving your course and your balance. You respond when the bike loses balance, destabilized perhaps by a hole or a bump: you change behavior, you react to recover and put the bike back on course. And you respond when the situation on the road changes: you avoid pedestrians, cars, and other bikes; you stop at junctions and red lights, and cycle more carefully in the rain.

Part of team leadership involves leading by example, but part involves guidance. For simple systems, guidance is programmatic, a matter of command and control. This doesn't work well for complex systems, and individuals and teams are complex systems indeed. Feedback is a guidance technique, but there's an art to it that goes beyond the simple presentation of the facts as you see them. To be effective, feedback also needs to be trusted, concrete, and constructive.

We generally don't consider people, no matter how upstanding they might be, to be objective sources of information in the way that inanimate objects and software tools are. When a piece of code fails a test or doesn't compile, we don't attribute this to a subjective judgment of the test or the emotional state of the compiler (unless we're having a bad day). When we receive feedback from people, we're more likely to hear what they say through a veil of emotions, cognitive biases, and relationships.

If the only feedback you offer is negative and corrective, it's likely to dampen anyone's spirits, independent of whether or not it's factually correct. Negative feedback is likely to breed mistrust and resentment. It's disempowering and unmotivating. The absence of any positive feedback, by implication, suggests that there's nothing the person is doing right.

Relentless feedback of any one form doesn't offer the guidance or build the trust that'll help you, the individual, or the team. This statement applies as much to unconditional positive feedback as it does to negative feedback. Positive feedback is psychologically necessary; otherwise, people feel like they're operating in a vacuum—the few humans who've ever been privileged to work in a literal, rather than figurative, vacuum know that support is a necessity, not an option—but there's a balance to be struck. Excessive and unwarranted positive feedback becomes saccharine and insincere.

Feedback should also be contextual and concrete. Saying someone's work is good is a pat on the back, but it's vague and there's little guidance, little they can take away from it beyond feeling congratulated. Specifically *what* about their work is good? Whether you're talking about someone overcoming a personal or technical challenge, meeting a goal, or fielding ideas, be specific. Unless you're specific, it's difficult for them to know *what* is good about what they did, in order that they learn from it, repeat it, and build on it.

The concept of learning and allowing someone else to do the learning highlights the weakness of negative feedback. Even without the question of self-esteem, pointing out that something isn't good isn't helpful, and in this case adding detail doesn't help. Saying something isn't good doesn't tell someone what *is* good. There's little they can learn from that feedback. It's like a no-entry sign on a one-way street: you're told which way you shouldn't go, but you aren't told which way you *should* go.

Negative feedback is often given in response to discovering a problem, but it isn't intrinsically problem-solving and constructive. To be constructive, you need to offer a concrete suggestion for improvement, or you need to make giving feedback part of a problem-solving conversation. If you want someone to learn, create the opportunity and environment for them to discuss and contribute; otherwise, the feedback becomes more about the person *giving* the feedback than the person *receiving* it. Feedback needs purpose and it should enable purpose.

Feedback, as a term, is often taken to be unidirectional; but as its engineering origins suggest, it's definitely about a relationship. It involves guidance and balance.

Roy's analysis

This is great advice. It's simple, yet many leaders aren't following it, because it's also hard to do. It requires the ability to sit face to face with a person and confront an uncomfortable subject head on.

From the point of view of a team's phase, I believe it would definitely fit into all phases. The type of feedback you'd choose to give at each phase might differ.

In the survival mode phase, if you're trying to get the team out of survival mode, and command-and-control leadership is active, feedback might be related to people doing things that are confusing the situation, people not contributing, or even explaining why someone must do an unpleasant task. "You have to stop working on X and focus only on Y," or "If there's one thing I need you to get done this week, it's X," are some things you're likely to hear from me in this phase.

In the learning phase, feedback would usually be related to any missing skills, or current challenges being faced by a team contributor. "You did great work on X. I could tell that was difficult for you," is something you might hear more often from me in this phase.

In the self-organization phase, feedback would be more about the decisions the team as a whole has made, or the overall goals for the team. "It's great that you've come up with this idea. Please come up with two more and then choose the one you'd like to try out first," and "How are we doing on our goals? Is there anything you need from me to get things done?" are some things you might hear from me at this phase.

Exercises

- In which phases of the team's maturity (survival mode, learning, self-organization) would this advice fit best? Would you implement feedback differently in each stage? Why?
- Consider the context of the six influence forces: personal ability, personal motivation, social ability, social motivation, environmental ability, and environmental motivation. If you implement the feedback advice listed here, which of the influence forces would you be using?

◆ ◆ ◆ ◆ ◆

KEVLIN HENNEY is an independent consultant and trainer with an interest in programming, patterns, practice, and process. He has been a columnist for a number of magazines and websites, not all of which have folded, and is the coauthor of *A Pattern Language for Distributed Computing* and *On Patterns and Pattern Languages,* two volumes in the *Pattern-Oriented Software Architecture* series (Wiley, 2007). He's also the editor of *97 Things Every Programmer Should Know* (O'Reilly, 2010). Kevlin speaks at conferences, lives online and in transit, and writes short fiction in what perhaps qualifies as his spare time.

12

Channel conflict into learning

by Dan North

Difference of opinion in high-performing teams isn't necessarily a bad thing. In fact, conflict is a necessary ingredient for learning teams. In his book *The Fifth Discipline* (Doubleday, 1990), Peter Senge describes the twin discourse activities of dialogue, where a team explores an idea from a number of perspectives, and discussion, where they attempt to reach consensus. If everyone agrees all the time, there isn't any stimulus for growth.

On the other hand, conflict between strong personalities can be difficult to manage and can cause factions or cliques within a team and eventually tear it apart. As a software team leader, it'll fall to you to make the big decisions: Which technologies should we adopt? Which of these competing frameworks should we choose? When the team senses change on the horizon, you'll find strong advocates for different alternatives, which can paralyze the team.

When I find a team blocked on a decision, I'll often suggest deferring the commitment by trying all the options simultaneously and letting the data inform the decision. On one occasion, a team leader asked me whether his experienced Java team should adopt Clojure or Scala as their "next generation" JVM language. The team had agreed they wanted to stay on the JVM but move beyond Java and had reached a stalemate over which direction to take. He was feeling pressured because, in his words, he had to make a decision imminently, both from a team health perspective and because stalling was beginning to impact their delivery. My answer surprised him:

"Should we go with Clojure or Scala?"

"Yes"

"Eh?"

There were six developers in his team, and I suggested they go with Clojure and Scala. And Java! At least for the next couple of weeks. One pair would learn Scala, one Clojure, and the third pair would stick with Java.

They'd all work on the same features, which means they'd be coding in a real domain rather than playing with code katas or tutorials, and within a couple of weeks they'd have some real data to make a decision with.

How easy was it to learn the language? How well was it suited to the problem at hand? How did each of the approaches compare with the others? How nicely did they integrate with the existing codebase? How important were each of these things in this context? They'd also have the Java solution as a control for comparison.

This approach uses an idea from the manufacturing industry called *set-based concurrent engineering*: several suppliers build the same thing—say, an airplane wing—in different ways, and after a while you choose one of them to take forward. You still pay the others—this exercise is at your expense rather than theirs—but it means that regardless of which you choose, you haven't lost any time. You trade efficiency for effectiveness: it's more expensive to get there, but you get there faster and you know you made a better decision. Many safety-critical industries mandate this approach for certain components.

The team leader added a nice twist to this. Halfway through, he got the pairs to switch around, and by the end of the experiment each pair had tried two of the languages. After several weeks, the team reached a strong consensus around one of the choices. They'd found it a better fit for their specific context, both in terms of the language itself and its libraries and toolchain. The team was unblocked and, what's more, they'd reached the decision as a team and learned about the alternatives along the way.

Roy's analysis

This is classic learning mode advice. There are several key points here:

- Conflict and discussion are part of the six influence forces (how peers react and pull each other in different directions).
- Parallel learning (set-based work) is a great technique, but it can't be done in survival mode.
- Unblocking a team might mean that the team doesn't know how to unblock itself, which we'll discuss in the next paragraphs.

What about the big goal, our mantra as leaders: to grow the team to the point of self-organization?

At a higher level, as a leader, conflict is an indication that the team is missing a skill: how to make a decision when there are multiple good choices. If, as a software team leader, it falls to you to make the big decisions, what does that indicate about the team?

The team leader becomes the decision-making bottleneck. The question then becomes this: "Why does the team leader have to be the decision maker? What skill does the team leader possess that the team doesn't?"

There are several possible influence forces that might be at play:

- Often, the team leader is the appointed technical entity with accountability for the state of the software and its sustainability;

therefore, they're responsible to make the decision. Of the six influence forces we discussed earlier in the book, this would fall under environmental motivation. Others might not want to make a decision in this case, because it's "not their place."

- The team leader knows (personal ability) about the set-based approach and can direct the team to follow that approach.
- The team culture might be "wait for someone else to decide" (social ability and social motivation), impelling the team leader to be the one to make the decision.

Assuming it's the first two and not the third, to grow the team into a more self-organizing state, several actions might need to be taken:

- Teach the team about this technique. Of the six influence forces, this falls under personal ability.
- At the organizational level, enable the team to follow the path of parallel learning when needed, without waiting for the team leader to suggest or instruct it. This can be as simple as "Guys, if I'm not here, next time something like this happens, feel free to take the same approach! You'll have my full backing even if management breathes down your neck, because this is the right thing to do." If management does continuously breathe down your neck, you might not be in learning mode, but in survival mode, and you need to push to get back into learning mode.

It's easy to focus on the day-to-day practices that optimize the team at a micro level, but attaining higher-level optimization by removing yourself as the bottleneck is key to make the team truly soar into new realms of productivity, loyalty, and passion.

Exercises

- What other types of events get your team "stuck" to the point where you have to intervene?

- What crucial skill do you bring to the table that results in the team depending on you to solve a problem?
- Is it a skill that you have, or is it a skill that they lack? For example, if people don't get along with each other, is it up to you to play mom and dad, or can you encourage people to speak with each other and try to solve their differences using some practices that you can teach them?

◆   ◆   ◆   ◆   ◆

DAN NORTH is an independent technology consultant who writes software and coaches teams and organizations in Agile and Lean methods. He believes in putting people first and writing simple, pragmatic software.

13

It's probably not a technical problem

by Bill Walters

I learned this from Jerry Weinberg, somewhere. The most difficult problems aren't technical problems. Typically, when you step back and get an objective look at the problem you're facing, chances are the real issue isn't a technical one; it's probably an irrational, subconscious soul-fart bubbling around inside somewhere, masked as a technical problem. It's not that this person doesn't understand how the wobbulator is supposed to work, it's that this person doesn't understand *and* there's a stigma or expectation that they should, and, therefore, the fear of being kicked out of the tribe is lurking somewhere beneath the surface.

Roy's analysis

Truer words have rarely been spoken. I'm a big fan of Jerry Weinberg myself, and I quote him in the book a couple of times!

Here's an attempt to "translate" Bill's note into this book's terms. This situation definitely falls into the "influence forces" discussion. If you're trying to understand why a person doesn't seem to get something and do it right, no matter how many times you've explained it, step back and look at the six influence forces.

Regarding personal ability and motivation, the person might *want* to do this task, but might not know *how* to accomplish it. But at the peer level (social motivation and ability), it might be that they react badly when a specific type of question is asked at the group level.

Helping people understand the way they feel about insufficiency might be the first step toward helping them overcome the fear of admitting that they don't know something.

Exercises

- Observe your team, and watch the interactions between people during the day.
- How do some people react to specific questions or notifications from other people when it's done face to face?
- Do you notice obvious cases where people should've said something but didn't?
- Why does that happen?
- Can you use the influence forces table in chapter 9 to start finding out?

◆ ◆ ◆ ◆ ◆

BILL WALTERS has been working in software and testing for a long time. He's attended the Jerry Weinberg Problem Solving Leadership workshop and read a number of his books and articles and can, therefore, be labeled a biased disciple.

14

Review the code

by Robert C. Martin (Uncle Bob)

One of the biggest mistakes that new software team leaders make is to consider the code written by the programmers as the private property of the author, as opposed to an asset owned by the team. This causes the team leaders to judge code based on its behavior rather than its structure. Team leaders with this dysfunction will accept any code as long as it does what it's supposed to do, regardless of how it's written.

> Indeed, such team leaders often don't bother to read other programmers' code at all. They satisfy themselves with the fact that the system works and divorce themselves from system structure. This is how you lose control over the quality of your system.

> Once you lose control, the software will gradually degrade into an unmaintainable morass. Estimates will grow, defect rates will climb, morale will decline, and eventually everyone will demand that the system be redesigned.

> A good team leader takes responsibility for the code structure as well as its behavior.

> A good team leader acts as a quality inspector, looking at *every* line of code written by any of the programmers under their lead.

A good team leader rejects a fair bit of that code and asks programmers to improve the quality of that code.

A good team leader maintains a vision of code quality.

They'll communicate that vision to the rest of the team by ensuring that the code they personally write conforms to the highest quality standards, and by reviewing all the other code in the system and rejecting the code that doesn't meet those exacting standards.

As teams grow, good team leaders will recruit lieutenants to help them with this review and enforcement task. The lieutenants review *all* the code, and the team leader falls back on reviewing *all* the code written by the lieutenants and spot-checking the code written by everyone else.

Code is a team asset, not personal property. No programmer should ever be allowed to keep their code private. Any other programmer on the team should have the right to improve that code at any time. And the team leader must take responsibility for the overall quality of the code.

The team leader must communicate and enforce a consistent vision of high quality and professional behavior.

Roy's analysis

Uncle Bob advocates that we influence the team by creating environmental rewards for writing good code and punishments for writing bad code, which can result in a positive outcome.

Here's an apparent paradox, though: you'd be hard pressed to find any team leader who disagrees with any piece of Uncle Bob's advice, and yet it's extremely difficult to find a team leader who practices it.

This is only an *apparent* paradox. Once we look at things from the *systems* viewpoint, it begins to make more sense. A good way to look at the systems view is to think about the influence forces as applied to team leaders who don't practice what they preach.

To start, let's choose one core behavior we'd like our team leader to embrace:

A good team leader acts as a quality inspector, looking at every line of code written by any of the programmers under their lead.

Let's look at each force, and try to imagine a scene from a real-life enterprise organization setting:

- *Personal ability*: Yes, that leader knows how to review code.
- *Personal motivation*: Yes, that leader would like to inspect everyone's code.

    This is where many people get stuck. Obviously leaders want to do this, and they think it's a good idea. What gives?

- *Social ability*: When the leader approaches a member of the team about the quality of the code, the member asks, "Should I refactor this instead of finishing this other urgent feature you told me to finish yesterday?"
- *Social motivation*: Other team leaders that are well respected by this leader, and have been working in the company for a long time, seem to pay no attention to code reviews. We could argue if they *should* be well respected, but that's a different paragraph.

OK, socially, when working with peers and colleagues, things seem to be getting a bit murky, and that team member has a good point: We're under some serious time pressure. You could say we're in survival mode; should we refactor that code?

On top of this, other team leaders seem to be doing fine (they do bellyache quite a bit about the quality of the products, but hey, don't we all?) without code quality looming over their heads.

Maybe the problem is more systemic. Let's look at the last two factors:

- *Environmental ability*: Are code reviews physically possible? Yes. The leader can see everyone's code easily if they choose to.

- *Environmental motivation*: Does the company reward the leader for *not* doing code reviews? Is there some *punishment* for taking the time to review code? In most companies, yes. There's time pressure to get code out the door, and quality takes a backseat. It's not necessarily good for the company, but customers don't usually understand this, and sometimes team leaders aren't committed to resisting this pressure.

These last two points complete our systems perspective. They point to a serious flaw: the team leader doesn't have the incentive to do the right thing—or, worse, is incentivized to do the wrong thing or else be berated by the managers.

Without solving this issue, as well as the social issues, it'll be difficult to see many team leaders taking that extra step toward the things they believe in.

Uncle Bob is asking team leaders to influence the team in the right direction by changing environmental forces, but team leadership might depend on other environmental forces already being in place, which is one of the reasons why many leaders today talk the talk but don't walk the walk.

Exercises

- What would you change in your workplace, at the system level, to enable team leaders to take responsibility for the overall quality of the code?
- What's the first step toward making this change happen? For example, "I'll set up a meeting with the CTO about this," or "I'll do a presentation to X folks about this" might be a good step, but your situation may need different steps first.

◆ ◆ ◆ ◆ ◆

ROBERT MARTIN (UNCLE BOB) has been a programmer since 1970. He's a
Master Craftsman at 8th Light Inc. and the author of many books, including *The Clean Coder* (Prentice Hall, 2011), *Clean Code* (Prentice Hall, 2008),
Agile Software Development (Pearson, 2002), and *UML for Java Programmers*
(Prentice Hall, 2003). He's a prolific writer and has published hundreds of
articles, papers, and blogs. He served as the editor-in-chief of *C++ Report*
and as the first chairman of the Agile Alliance.

15

Document your air, food, and water

by Travis Illig

Think about all of the things you need to know when you're new to a team. There are a lot of things, right?

- Where's the source code repository?
- Which tools need to be installed on your developer environment?
- What're the steps to build the product?
- Is there a pattern for how the code is laid out in the repository?
- How are tasks tracked?
- What's the task branch pattern in the repository?
- Where's the continuous integration server?
- Are there any specific development methodologies that should be followed?

This is, from a peer mentoring perspective, the "air, food, and water" for the group.

It's the stuff you need to know in order to basically get around. Many times, the answers to these questions aren't documented anywhere. It's "tribal knowledge."

People "know" what needs to be done, and if you don't know, you ask the group. That sort of approach might work well in a small group that doesn't change a lot, but what about in a larger group?

Does everyone know? Or is there a slightly different understanding of how things work from person to person? And what about new team members?

Document basic team information

It's a good idea to *document your air, food, and water* in a central location that's accessible to everyone. Keep a "team FAQ" sheet that has the answers to all these questions, and make sure everyone knows where it is. It doesn't have to be reams of heavy documentation, but it should contain enough to clearly answer the questions.

Why document?

Enable team members to help themselves

It's generally understood[1] that "quick questions" that cause team members to task-switch are not as "free" as you might think.[2] Having a place that folks can go to answer simple questions reduces context switches, particularly when there are newer members on the team.

Give new team members confidence in the team

The last time you joined a team, how was the experience? Did it seem a little jarring, or was it smooth? When you're new to a team, it's like meeting a person for the first time ... and you only get one chance to make a first impression. Wouldn't it be nice to join a team and have the reassurance that there's a plan and a simple document

---

[1] See Jeff Atwood's "The Multitasking Myth," *Coding Horror*, September 27, 2006, https://blog.codinghorror.com/the-multi-tasking-myth.

[2] See Kermit Pattison's "Worker, Interrupted: The Cost of Task Switching," *Fast Company*, July 28, 2008, http://mng.bz/vU68.

that lays out everything you need to know to get going? If you saw that, wouldn't you gain a little confidence in the team?

Provide visibility into your team

If there are other people or teams in your company that are interested in seeing how you're doing things, maybe to learn something from your team, having a document makes it easy for them to see how things are done and understand what they're looking at.

How do you get started? How do you maintain this document?

Find a location, and tend the document

Find a central place on your company's network where you can store the document such that everyone has access to it. Maybe it's a wiki. Maybe it's a SharePoint site. Maybe it's a simple file share. As long as everyone has access to it, it's perfect.

Document as questions arise

As people have questions about how the team works—where the source code is, and so on—refer them to the document. If the answer isn't there, consider adding the answer to the document and providing the document to the person asking the question. Eventually you'll have a document with the answers to the most frequently asked questions about the team.

Pass it by exiting team members

Team members come in, and team members move on. Before a team member moves on from the team, part of the knowledge transfer should be having them review the document and fill in applicable answers. There may be some things the team member was responsible for that no one else knows about.

Give it to new team members

When a new member comes on board, give them the document as a way to get them set up. It'll quickly become apparent if the information on the document is incomplete. When incomplete/incorrect information is encountered, have the new team member work with the team to find out the correct information and update the document.

Update as changes occur

As changes are made in the way the team works, update the document to reflect them. There shouldn't be an overwhelming amount of information to maintain, but the doc does need to be a living entity, like your team is.

Keep your document fairly lightweight and easy to maintain

If it's too thick or complex, or if information's repeated in multiple places throughout, people will skip updating the document and eventually it'll become stale. You don't want that—you want it to be easy when it's time to update: *simple, simple, simple.*

It doesn't take much, and it pays off in spades. Why not start today?

Roy's analysis

One immediate value to this practice is that it can help reduce bus factors in your team.

I once had a team member who was the only person who knew how to clean up disk space on a build machine when it filled up. He used a special script he made a long time ago, and only he knew where it was located and how to run it. By documenting that stuff in a shared wiki, it was easy to then point people to the wiki page if and when it was needed, regardless of if he was there. Bus factors are huge risks to the team and any project you're working on, and knowledge sharing in a safe place that's easily accessible and searchable is a safety net preventing the risk that only one person possesses unique knowledge.

It's possible that a lot of unforeseen work your team might be doing has the root cause that they're reinventing the wheel, or not sharing information well enough. Creating a script to clean the disk when someone has already created such a script is wasteful.

Acting on this advice can prevent situations that risk your team devolving back into (or keep the team in) survival mode.

This advice might belong in the learning phase, because it might require time you need to handle getting out of survival mode.

◆ ◆ ◆ ◆ ◆

TRAVIS ILLIG is a .NET developer who enjoys the art of solving problems with technology. He currently is a Senior Software Developer with Fiserv, working on next-generation online banking products. He holds a BS in Computer Science from Portland State University and is a Microsoft Certified Solutions Developer (MCSD) for .NET. Travis can be contacted through his blog at www.paraesthesia.com.

16

Appraisals and agile don't play nicely

by Gary Reynolds

Appraisals, performance reviews, 360 feedback, evaluations—call them what you will—have been present in organizations in one form or another for over 100 years. Over this time, the process has taken a number of different forms, depending on the current trends and the size of the organization.

I personally have experience with written evaluations where the employee has no input, various rating systems where both employees and managers get to rate the individual, and written appraisals where the employee makes comments on their own performance that are used as the basis for further discussion. Some systems have been directly linked to pay and promotion opportunities, whereas others have been explicitly decoupled.

One thing they all have in common is that they focus on the individual, their performance, and what they've accomplished since the last review period. They encourage the individual to take credit for themselves and to compete against the other people on their team for recognition and a limited pot of money when it comes to bonuses and salary increases.

I'd suggest that this is in direct conflict with the adoption and use of agile frameworks within the organization. Think about it:

- Agile emphasizes teamwork and cooperation in order to successfully deliver a product, with individuals being prepared to take on any task that needs doing in order to complete the iteration and get to "done." Individual accountability, as valued by the traditional appraisal system, implies that individuals should be interested in taking the juiciest or most challenging tasks for themselves in order to prove their worth and progress within the organization.
- Agile emphasizes the forming of self-organizing teams that direct and manage their own work, whereas appraisals involve the setting of objectives that traditionally come from the manager.
- Agile processes emphasize constant process improvement. Although this can be done alongside traditional appraisals, appraisals are geared more toward making individual or process changes at review time.

Is there a case for abolishing appraisals altogether in an agile environment? Well, perhaps. The challenge is that individuals within an organization expect and deserve feedback on their performance.

Perhaps a step in the right direction would be for team leaders to make the appraisal process itself more agile and encourage an environment where the annual review is replaced or supplemented with a system of continuous feedback and learning, where individuals—in line with agile—are empowered to self-organize their own career development. Here are some ideas to get you started:

- Build learning and career development into individual user stories, perhaps in the form of a specific task that involves team members expanding their business domain knowledge. Alternatively, include time for learning tasks into your velocity calculations to increase the value of each team member to the organization by expanding their skillset in a way that's relevant to their immediate task. Let the individuals drive and organize this learning process as they would a normal development task.

- Encourage pairing (pair-programming, for example) on tasks that help individuals to learn from those more experienced.
- Include team member feedback sessions as part of your iteration retrospective process, where you can directly discuss what people have learned.
- Encourage individuals, on an iteration-by-iteration basis, to maintain a body of evidence that can be directly referenced at formal appraisal time. This will reduce the time taken to plan and perform the appraisal and encourages the recording of tasks at the time they happen—when they're most relevant.

What else can you think of?

Roy's analysis

Think about the influence forces and the environmental motivation force. That's the force that relates to company rewards and punishments for specific behaviors.

In essence this note shows us that yearly performance reviews can badly influence employee behaviors by *rewarding* selfish work and knowledge hoarding. The note also discusses how we can reward different kinds of behavior by changing how we ask our team to do things (pairing) and rewarding the right behaviors (measuring learning at individual and team levels).

Exercises

- How does your company or environment reward good or bad practices? For example, do people end up financially advantaged (bonus) by shipping poor quality, quickly? Do people get berated by their manager for refactoring instead of working on new features?

- List at least two good behaviors and two bad behaviors that you see people do, and how they're rewarded or punished by the environment (mentally, financially, or in some other way).

◆ ◆ ◆ ◆ ◆

GARY REYNOLDS is a Development Manager for a global software company, with particular expertise in transitioning teams from traditional software development practices to more agile ways of working.

17

Leading through learning: the responsibilities of a team leader

by Cory Foy

I was honored when Roy asked me to explore the topic of team leadership. It's an interesting topic because it can cover such a broad array of factors.

We could cover the usual things, such as servant leadership, impediment removal, or motivation, but there's one thing that intrinsically sets great leaders apart from mediocre ones. To get there, we should first discuss the responsibility of a team member.

One of the things that excites me the most about the Software Craftsmanship movement is a shift of responsibility. Frequently we, as developers, have set out with the ingrained feeling that it's our organization's responsibility to help us grow and succeed. This was true, to some extent, in the early days—great programmers stayed with great companies for a long time.

Growth was something you expected when you were hired. You could look forward to staying with the company, putting in your best, and getting rewarded upon retirement with the knowledge that you'll be cared for in return.

Those days are gone. I don't know of any colleagues who've taken a job with a company thinking they'd be there for 20 or 30 years. That seemingly coincides with the mantra of "Here today, gone tomorrow," which some organizations practice. That further means that, if we can't even be sure that our jobs are still going to be here, we certainly can't expect that it's a given that organizations will help us grow.

As a part of the Craftsmanship movement, we've declared that we shouldn't expect to be gaining knowledge from organizational initiatives or in the course of our role on a team. In fact, the core of the movement is that developers need to be taking responsibility for their own careers—learning, teaching, mentoring, speaking.

In this book, Roy explores the questions each team leader should ask themselves. One key question, perhaps the hardest question for many leads to answer, is this: Is my team better than it was last week?

This approach is what has set my preferred leads above others. It doesn't matter which industry—I saw it from software team leads as much as fire captains and other industries I've been involved with. How do I create learning opportunities that enable my team to grow?

This past weekend I went to BarCamp Tampa Bay (http://barcamptampabay.org) and got to see Steven Bristol (http://b.lesseverything.com) speak about starting up a company. He mentioned how feedback loops affect growth. If you're single, and go up to someone and ask them out, one of three things will happen:

- They'll say yes.
- They'll say no (or some variant, like slapping you upside the head.)
- They'll turn around and walk away without saying a word.

Out of the three, which will you learn the most from? Which will cause you to grow the most? Which will leave you scratching your head?

Imagine now that you're a developer on a team. You email your team lead and ask about taking on a new initiative for the team. The next afternoon an announcement is made that one of the senior developers is going to be working on the initiative you emailed about.

Baffling, huh? Imagine if, instead, the team lead emailed you back and told you that they have concerns because you haven't been involved with FooBar, and Senior Joe is going to take this initiative but will work closely with you so that you can jump on the next one.

Or, imagine the team lead replied and said, "Go for it," and offered guidelines to measure your progress. Let's say you took that and failed miserably, but, because of the team involvement, others were able to pick up the ball and help you get it done.

That's what you want from a team lead. This, in many ways, is the essence of leadership: providing opportunities for people to fall, but always within the context of the safety net of the team. Motivating not by fear or finance, but by passion that comes with the knowledge that the team is always greater than any one developer. It's turning your day-to-day interactions into chances for growth and learning, and ultimately building a learning organization.[1]

Team leadership is about setting aside your ego, your pride, to be able to go out and help others. Effective team leads aren't generally the rock star developers who put in 70-hour weeks because they're hard core. They're solid technical leaders—and solid *social* leaders.

---

[1] See Scott Bellware's blog entry "Learning Culture," December 27, 2008, http://mng.bz/ Qi11.

For example, Scott Bellware had an article on the Chief Engineer role[2] in which he described the responsibilities and qualities of the chief engineer at Toyota. These included

- Voice of the customer
- Architecture
- Exceptional engineering skills
- A hard-driving teacher, motivator, and disciplinarian, yet a patient listener
- An exceptional communicator
- Always ready to get his or her hands dirty

If you're thinking about leading a team or finding yourself thrust into that role, ask yourself—are you growing? Are you seeking opportunities for yourself? For the team? Are you listening—truly listening—to what your team's telling you? Or are you constantly impatient for them to finish speaking so you can tell them the *right* answer? Most importantly, what actions are you taking today to make your developers—your team—better one week, one month, one year from now?

In the answers to those questions lies the growth path for you as a leader. Keep growing, keep questioning, and keep learning—and your team will too.

Roy's analysis

This practice can and should be used as a fundamental way to approach the learning phase in a team.

The feedback aspect is interesting because you can map it to a couple of the influence forces I mentioned earlier in the book. When you give feedback to a team member on their behavior or actions, you influence them in at least three ways:

---

[2] Scott Bellware, "Chief Engineer," December 17, 2008, http://mng.bz/wJnJ.

- *Social ability*—How people react to your actions.
- *Social motivation*—Assuming they respect you, then your line of thinking on improvement will affect their line of thinking.
- *Environmental motivation*—Your role as an appointed leader also signifies that from the organization's standpoint, it's recommended to learn new things, which is what the organization rewards. This can backfire if there are opposing rewards or influences.

CORY FOY is an agile coach and developer living in Bayonet Point, Florida. He's currently helping product teams become leaner in their approaches to building product through the focused use of both craftsmanship and agile practices and principles. Prior to his current role, Cory worked with teams around the globe bringing agile and development best practices to Microsoft customers as a Senior PFE. He has also been involved in several start-up organizations where delivering high value while keeping the code clean is vital. When not spending time with his wife and two girls, Cory enjoys working as the global community liaison for the Scrum Alliance, speaking at conferences and user groups, and playing guitar, drums, or whatever he can get his hands on. He can be found at www.cornetdesign .com or on Twitter at https://twitter.com/cory_foy.

18

Introduction to the Core Protocols

by Yves Hanoulle

Roy asked me if I wanted to write about the Core Protocols (www
.mccarthyshow.com/online/). I'll start by explaining where these protocols
originated.

> This story starts in 1995. Jim McCarthy wrote *Dynamics of Software Devel-opment* (Microsoft Press, 1995). After this book was well received in
> the software community (I see it as one of the predecessors of agile),
> Jim and his wife Michele decided to leave Microsoft to hold work-shops on team-building. They designed these workshops to be experi-mental. The course wasn't presented like a typical class; it was a
> simulated one-week project. Part of the assignment was for the stu-dents to come up with their own team rules.
>
> After a year Jim and Michele realized that some team patterns kept get-ting great results. They decided to write these rules down and give them
> to the students attending the next workshop. They've done that for the
> last 13 years. These patterns are now called the Core Protocols.
>
> Some—heck, *most*—of these rules feel strange at first. You might
> think, *this will never work...*
>
> - In my company
> - In my country

- With my wife
- With my kids
- In my team

I'm asking you to suspend your disbelief and try out a few of these in a safe environment. You don't have to believe in the sea to get wet. You only have to get in.

In this note, I'll cover the Check-In Protocol portion of the Core Protocols. One of the most effective and, consequently, one of the most controversial protocols is Check-In.

In presentations, when I ask the audience, "Who has worked with a colleague who hides emotions?" almost everyone raises their hand. When I then ask if this has hindered productivity at work, almost all the hands stay up.

Yet a lot of people are still convinced that showing their emotions at work isn't "professional."

I find that the Check-In Protocol offers a powerful way to express emotions in a mature way, both at work and in my personal life. During a check-in, we state how we feel using four basic emotions: mad, glad, sad, and afraid.

Let me give you an example. I'm checking in:

> *I'm GLAD that Roy has asked me to write these guest posts. I'm AFRAID, too. I'm GLAD I can ask for help. I'm AFRAID that the power of the protocols can only be understood by using them. I'm AFRAID, SAD that people will turn away without trying them. I'm GLAD to know that some people will probably accept my invitation to try them. I'm IN.*

In this example, I used the protocol to the letter. When I use the protocols with people not familiar with the Core, I might say something like this:

> *Hello, welcome to this training, I'm Yves Hanoulle. I'm glad to see a packed room. I'm afraid that this puts pressure on me to make it*

great. That's OK because I've done this a lot of times. I'm mad because my replacement phone doesn't work here in Canada. I'm sad because delivering this workshop means I'll miss my kids for 5 days.

If you think that this won't work in your company, in your country, or with your spouse, then you aren't alone.

I had a similar reaction about using the protocol with my oldest son. I was having a chat with Michele (McCarthy). She asked me to try check-in with him. I told her that he was three and a half years old and that I thought he was too young. We finished the conversation with my promise that I'd try it. I was still convinced it wouldn't work. The next day Joppe came home with a card from school with these four Check-In Protocol emotions on it. I realized *I* was the reason it wasn't working; *he* already understood the four emotions. I've been using it with him ever since.

Using check-in with Joppe has taught me a lot. One night he said, "I'm MAD, SAD that the babysitter will be here, and you guys are going out." At that time, my partner and I went out to dinner every Thursday. It was a Thursday, but that day we weren't going to go, and we hadn't told him. Typically, we only told him when we were going out on the day we did. He'd already made the connection, though, that Thursday equals babysitter. I realized that evening that Joppe might only be four years old, but he was much cleverer than I was giving him credit for.

Now for a work story.

One morning I had an argument with my partner before leaving for work. The discussion was stuck in my head as I drove. On top of that, a crazy truck driver almost drove me off the road. When I arrived at work, I realized I wasn't my rational self because of these two events. When I came in I told my colleagues, "Sorry if I overreact a little today; I had a discussion at home before leaving; I'm still puzzled about some of the things we said to each other. I'm also mad about a crazy truck driver who drove me off the road." Right then my colleague gave me 10 minutes of slack time. Also, because I'd checked in, I immediately forgot about what had happened. I didn't remember until I got back in my car that evening. Without checking in, I would've been stuck on those thoughts and feelings all day, and my productivity would've been a fraction of normal.

I propose you try the Check-In Protocol at work and at home, and see how much more bandwidth you can create in your communication lines.

As a bonus, once you're skilled at using it, it keeps working over email or chat.

Roy's analysis

The Core Protocols are still a mystery to me. I admit I haven't tried the Check-In Protocol. Writing this analysis feels a little strange ... and uncomfortable.

Here I am, writing the second edition of this book, after a few years of forcing my wife and three kids to travel the world through countries that took us completely out of our comfort zone (Israel, Norway, USA East Coast and West Coast), and yet I'm still afraid to try this one little practice.

Add that to the not-so-short list of things I'm still afraid of trying, and you can see why I feel a bit of a hypocrite. Maybe that's not a bad thing.

The key to learning is to get out of our comfort zone and become uncomfortable, and yet I find that this feeling is a large part of the human condition (Google "Imposter syndrome"). Once you get over this feeling, it's comforting to know that at any point in time you can *choose* to get out of yet another comfort zone, and jump into one of the many ravines that you know await you, lurking. Many rivers to cross, the road's the goal, that sort of thing.

In a sense, this note is about discovering a possible ravine you might want to challenge yourself to dive into one day, after you've maneuvered ravines of your own.

It's on my bucket list to try, but not soon. I have several other ravines I plan to dive into before that, and you should have a small list in your head, too.

Exercises

- What ravines do you have planned for yourself in the coming weeks? Months? Years?
- Are they truly ravines? How do you know? How much does it scare you to try them? How much risk is there? What'll you possibly lose besides your ego?

◆ ◆ ◆ ◆ ◆

YVES HANOULLE is a virtual project coach. You can reach him at his training company (www.paircoaching.net/) or follow him on Twitter (http://twitter.com/yveshanoulle/).

19

Change your mind: your product is your team

by Jose Ramón Díaz

You should change your mind about what you're building when you become a project manager or team leader (as a boss).

Forget your product. Look at your team. Suddenly, you don't have to worry about technical decisions or pretty interfaces. You must realize that the basics of your work have changed. My own inspiration is the mantra "team equals product":

The product will be as good as your team is.

The behavior of your team will determine the qualities of the product.

So your product as project manager is the team. Invest in the team. This will change your efforts profoundly and redirect them toward helping the team grow.

I first read that idea in the book *Software for Your Head* (Addison Wesley Professional, 2002), by Jim and Michelle McCarthy. This was annoying and shocking for me.

Now I believe every little effort you make to improve your team infuses the products they create. You must be ready for that. Your behavior must change to let your people do their best.

If you've been assigned as project manager recently, start studying again! (Take a little advice: read, and read a lot!) You have no more technology-related problems.

I love Alistair Cockburn's comment: "If you *don't* know anything about human behavior, you know very little about software development."

So stop and think about your previous work: do you really know something about people and their behaviors? Start changing your focus from product to team, and from technology to people.

Pay attention to people, and identify the phase your team is in and what it needs in order to evolve. Find the right leadership for that phase. Admit you can't become the one and only *leader*, but you can be that person who turns mediocre teams into great teams: a great *manager*.

If you keep thinking about building products, these will only be as good as you're able to manage and control your team. But if you facilitate the emergence of the full potential of your team, the product will be enhanced and enriched by many people and their synergy.

Roy's analysis

This note eloquently states one of the main points of this book. If you look back at the Team Leader Manifesto presented in chapter 1, you see ideas about focusing as much on people as on software, and understanding that great teams make great software.

Whenever we're faced with a tough question, "What do I do now?" the guiding principle should be "What pushes my team closer to self-organization and being able to solve their own problems?"

- In survival mode, decisions are based on getting the team out of survival mode (even if that means focusing on current actions and removing over-commitment).
- In learning mode, decisions are based on what removes you and other bus factors from key points, so the team can flow in their implementation of solutions to problems and ultimately reach a pure self-organizing state.
- In self-organization mode, it's about keeping things flowing and making sure that, if they degenerate again, you take the right steps to correct that situation.

If software is a beam of light that's projected on a wall, then your team is the flashlight that shines that light. To change the light—its focus, its texture, its colors—work on the flashlight, not the wall, and not the beam.

Bad teams produce bad software. Even potentially *good* teams that handle pressure badly produce bad software. Teams that know how to handle what you throw at them, and know what to do when they *don't* know what to do, are the ones that make great software. But that takes a team with the skills to do this.

◆ ◆ ◆ ◆ ◆

JOSE RAMÓN DÍAZ (http://najaraba.blogspot.com/) has been developing software for more than 10 years, and now he shares agile principles and practices as the best way to improve organizations and teams. He's interested in encouraging teams to become effective and efficient, while also enjoying their work.

20

Leadership and the mature team

by Mike Burrows

Roy's second chapter about the three team phases rings true in my experience as a team member, project leader, and development manager, but still it touches a red button of mine! I'm grateful to Roy for his gracious offer to let me respond.

My red button? I worry about the Agile community's recent focus on self-management. Don't get me wrong; self-management's a good thing, but in its current popular usage it has two problems:

- It fails to satisfactorily capture the powerful concept (borrowed from the study of systems) of self-organization.
- There seems to be a move in the community to minimize the role of leadership.

Self-organization's at the heart of agile methods; indeed, it's the 11th of the 12 principles behind the Agile Manifesto. Definitions vary, but, in this context, it describes the ability of a system (here, the project team) to create ways to increase its effectiveness.

Looking at the team from the outside, we see *emergence*—new behaviors arising without external intervention. In the Scrum con-text this might happen as a result of team retrospectives (the 12th principle)

162

or through the individual contributions of team members. Either way, it's important to recognize that some of these new behaviors (or innovations) may be highly nonstandard.

Whether from within or without, leadership takes the team to places it'd otherwise never have reached, perhaps never even have considered. This can be in terms of the team's internal structures or its external goals, but, in the absence of leadership, it's a rare thing for a team to take itself out of its comfort zone, to redefine its approach to the outside world, perhaps even to completely reinvent itself.

Here's the paradox: good leadership encourages emergence, but the leader must also be ready to take the team out of the niche it has carved out for itself. Yes, self-management is needed at every level (without it, the leader only has time for management), but we need the humility to recognize its limits. Now, there's true maturity!

Roy's analysis

This note rings true, in that I've led teams that were self-organizing, but yet were unaware that there were things they didn't know, but needed to know:

> *Reports that say that something hasn't happened are always interesting to me, because as we know, there are known knowns; there are things we know we know. We also know there are known unknowns; that is to say we know there are some things we do not know. But there are also unknown unknowns—the ones we don't know we don't know. And if one looks throughout the history of our country and other free countries, it is the latter category that tends to be the difficult one.*
> —Donald Rumsfeld

Insofar as a team is aware of the things it knows, and even of the things it knows it doesn't know, a team will always have unknown unknowns; and without some outside catalyst to learning, a team can stay unaware of possible improvements.

I feel that a leader in a self-organizing phase has the primary responsibility to watch out for when a team might believe they're self-organizing, when, in fact, they're missing some important skill or knowledge, and to push them into a learning phase to start learning the missing skill.

I once led a team of pros. They all knew what they were doing, but they were operating in a narrow field of software. Main SCM: Configuration Management. The organization didn't know it, but that team needed to transcend its current abilities and start supporting more than source control and builds. I pushed them into a much larger view of software processes, including automation, testing, cloud activities, monitoring, security, and more.

The team wasn't aware these were activities that somehow would need to sit in their lap, or that they'd benefit the organization. That also means not everyone's going to love all these changes, and people might feel that their expertise might be "thrown away" in order to work on things outside their expertise. This is usually an indicator that people are out of their comfort zone. It's not a happy place, but it's a passionate place and an important one, and it needs to happen for a team to grow and transcend its current abilities.

◆ ◆ ◆ ◆ ◆

MIKE BURROWS (http://twitter.com/asplake) is well known to the Kanban community through his definitive book *Kanban from the Inside* (Blue Hole Press, 2014) and his blog (http://positiveincline.com). Now a consultant, interim manager, and trainer, he has been a global development manager and IT director, and was for a time responsible for Kanban curriculum development at Lean Kanban University.

21

Spread your workload

by John Hill

During my many years of experience as a team lead (albeit only recently in software development), I've seen other team leads "flog their workhorses." In many team environments, there will be members who are less likely to willingly accept tasks they don't enjoy—the *complainers* (they kick up a stink)—and those who get their heads down and complete any task that you give them—the *reliables*. I've seen many team leaders, including me in my early years, give the less fun jobs to the reliables, as there's less chance of resistance and conflict.

In the short term, this strategy may work in your favor, but there are some repercussions:

- The team as a whole may begin to pass work off to the reliables.
- The reliables will eventually burn out.
- The reliables will become frustrated, and you'll more than likely lose their respect.
- Internal conflict will arise because the reliables will separate themselves from the complainers.

The solution involves sharing the load equally. If you gave a "boring" task to Member A today, give the next boring task to Member B—

regardless of whether they complain. This will build up a culture of equality, with every team member having their share of learning opportunities.

Roy's analysis

The solution's nice. But to paraphrase Jerry Weinberg: many leaders like to take the money but not do all the hard parts about leadership. And I'm certain that this note's giving great advice that many leaders will find hard to follow specifically because it requires a little bit of conflict. For many leaders, conflict is the opposite of what a safe work environment looks like, but it's essential to get out of that comfort zone and realize that conflict is necessary, as described in *The Five Dysfunctions of a Team* by Patrick Lencioni (Jossey-Bass, 2002).

By getting out of our comfort zone and doing this thing we find hard to do (asking things of people who don't like to do them), we also grow ourselves. We see what happens when we push a boundary. We learn more about ourselves and other people, and we see what happens when certain things are being triggered in our work environment. We become better because we gain more perspective: different approaches to things bring experience that we can use in our work. Not to mention that we play fair, and make the team play fair, which builds loyalty.

One more question to be asked is, "Why is the team leader *assigning* things to specific members?" You'd expect members of a self-organizing team to select tasks for themselves. This is a clue that the team isn't self-organizing, or it's not treated as such.

Whether that makes sense or not remains unknown. Perhaps it's the right thing to do when the team's in survival mode. In learning mode, it might still make sense to assign tasks to team members, but specifically to learn new skills and get them out of their comfort zones. It wouldn't make sense to give tasks to people who're masters of these skills, but who serve as bus factors for that knowledge in the team; while you assign a DB maintenance task (something simple) to a member with less DB experience, in order that they learn.

In learning mode, you can also think a bit more "meta" and teach the team to pick and choose their own tasks, based on how uncomfortable it makes them. Teach a team to get itself out of the comfort zone, and you've created a team of leaders.

A self-organizing team already knows how to choose their own tasks. It wouldn't make sense to assign tasks to team members.

◆　◆　◆　◆　◆

JOHN HILL is a .NET Team Leader/Senior Developer for a small Australian CMS software development company.

22

Making your team manage their own work

by Lior Friedman

I was reading the previous note in this book (at the time, it didn't include Roy's analysis), and it got me thinking. It took me a while to understand why I felt that it isn't quite right. And then it hit me: the game of the team lead choosing who does what isn't worth playing. It's better to avoid the problem to begin with, and the best way to do this is to let the team decide who does what.

If you want to become a great team leader, you need to stop being the team task dispatcher. Normally, a group of people will do a better job at this than a single person. Your job as the team leader is to allow this; make your team self-manage.

If your team isn't there yet, it's a good goal to strive for and invest effort in. The first step is to stop deciding for the team. As long as you decide who does what, the team won't take charge of its work. After all, why should they worry when you do this for them?

I know this isn't easy to accomplish, but here's what works for me when I approach this problem.

Making your team manage their own work

Explain the new "rules" to the team. When expecting someone to start doing something new, I find it usually helps to state my expectation. The first thing I do is to tell them that, from now on, I expect them to divide the work between them. I also say that if they find it difficult, I'm willing to help.

Teach them how to do it

After the team understands the new expectation, I like to make sure they know how to accomplish it. In this case, I'll explain how I think tasks should be divided. I'll give tips and advice on how to balance the work, how to make sure everything's done as fast as possible, and what I'll expect to see.

I find that visualizing a problem goes a long way toward solving it. In this case, I devise a way to put all the work tasks into a single visible place. My preferred technique uses a physical task board, but an Excel list works as well. The same mechanism can be used to track how the team is doing.

Remember that, like any new skill, mistakes will be made along the way. That's okay. Mistakes are what people learn from. Don't try to prevent them; just make sure the damage isn't too bad and people learn from the mistakes.

Roy's analysis

This is a great addition to the previous note. It goes without saying that this firmly belongs in the learning phase.

◆　◆　◆　◆　◆

LIOR FRIEDMAN is an Agile coach and Software Craftsman with more than 15 years of experience. In recent years he consulted and trained teams worldwide on how to improve software development. Specifically, he helps companies adopt agile software development processes and teaches development teams how to improve the quality of their code by using advanced techniques like TDD, BDD, and other agile practices.

23

Go see, ask why, show respect

by Horia Slușanschi

The best way to help your team serve their clients better, and to achieve and sustain a culture of continuous improvement, is to start by showing them deep respect.

How can you best show respect? Consider Jim Womack's excellent advice in his collection of essays *Gemba Walks* (Lean Enterprise Institute, 2011).

You do this by challenging their thinking about the current work process, asking lots of open, probing questions to uncover the root causes of current impediments. No process is ever perfect, but you can focus on helping the team to discover what its key constraint is at any particular moment, and then devise countermeasures to remedy it.

The *key constraint* is the area in which an improvement will show the biggest bang for the buck when measured across the entire system, improving the overall flow of the work process, and likely reducing cycle time and waste, with less overburden or absurdity involved.

By engaging your team in problem-solving, you show them that you choose not to attempt to solve the problem alone. You trust them to be best positioned to come up with the most promising improvement ideas, as they're closest to the work being done and have all the facts in hand. As a team leader, you truly respect your team's knowledge and their dedication to finding the best answer.

Still, team members can't quite do it all alone because they're often too close to the issue to appreciate its full context. They may avoid tough questions about the nature of the work and the reasoning behind certain inefficient practices. By showing mutual respect, better countermeasures can be devised, the team can derive more pride in the quality of their work, and everyone can enjoy a more satisfying journey of professional accomplishment.

To better serve your team, work to understand yourself better, assessing your own strengths and weaknesses. Strive to become aware of your team's characteristics as well, sensing their professional and emotional development needs. Be ready to adapt your leadership, coaching, and mentoring style to suit the team's current spot on its journey to professional mastery.

Roy's analysis

This great note belongs firmly in the learning and self-organization phases. It also emphasizes (indirectly) two important risk aversions:

- Avoiding becoming a bottleneck by getting the team to make decisions about important questions
- Avoiding treating a team in learning/self-organizing mode as if they're in survival mode

We also encourage team spirit and loyalty by giving people more control over their destiny.

One thing that I failed to mention earlier in the book is that self-organizing teams can only go so far. It sometimes takes a person who's a bit removed from a situation to clearly see a path ahead and ask the right questions. A code review should be done by someone who didn't write the code. It's helpful that some onlooker can make sure the team sees the forest for the trees.

The next step is to ask, "Why am I the only one who may know how to ask the right questions?" At that point, start teaching the team the skill of stepping out of the current box and asking the right questions, which brings the team one level up to a meta thinking state that can awaken when the need arises.

When that happens, the leader is needed less as the "objective outsider who asks smart questions." The team should eventually grow to be a team of leaders, each of whom can ask important questions that might come from an objective perspective.

What does the leader do? Make sure that the team knows how to ask questions in order to stay on top of their game. Leaders are fallible in believing they know how to ask the right questions. An important leadership skill is to ask, "Am I still asking the right questions?"

At some point, leaders need outside feedback, from true outsiders. That's why it's common to have coaches in high levels of management. Good leaders know that they might be blindly asking the wrong questions. The question then becomes, "Am I asking the wrong questions?" The answer has to come from feedback from the outside.

This is the kind of support a leader can give to a self-organizing team, who might *think* they're asking the right questions, but aren't.

Exercises

- Are you and your team asking the right questions?
- How can your team know if they are?
- How can you know if you are?
- Find an outsider you can confer with, whom you trust, to give you feedback on the questions you're asking yourself daily regarding your team.

◆ ◆ ◆ ◆ ◆

HORIA SLUŞANSCHI is a passionate agile coach, serving as the leader of the HP Agile Mentoring Office and the HP Software Engineering Profession. He has written software of various kinds, from firmware for devices, to compilers for supercomputers, and all sorts of business systems in between, for more than 25 years. Horia holds a PhD in Computer Science, is a trained Lean Six Sigma Black Belt practitioner, and holds various other certifications and memberships with professional associations. His calling lies in growing more accomplished leaders, helping teams to achieve amazing results.

24

Keep developers happy, reap high-quality work

by Derek Slawson

While at Northwestern Memorial Hospital, I was an unofficial team leader trying to advance our team forward during a unique situation: we were a side project for our manager, who was largely absent due to other responsibilities. He had less and less time for us as the months went on (a scenario that was slowly rectified). Previously, I was the official manager of a small development team at another company, although, admittedly, I learned more about the needs of a development team in a situation with no manager than I did in my prior position. I have a natural inclination toward best practices and learning, and I tried to fill the vacuum on our team as much as possible.

One of the most important lessons I learned is that if you keep your developers happy and motivated, they'll consequently do some of their best work and will contribute to the betterment of the team and the organization. The tricks involved with keeping them motivated may initially seem counterintuitive to developers and/or management.

First and foremost, you need an agreed-upon team coding standard, but then you can't neglect it. You need to thoroughly enforce it. Although some developers may find that this gets nit-picky, it ultimately ensures your code base follows the same standards and patterns throughout, making it easier to maintain and train new staff in the future. This has the added benefit of enabling your developers to quickly turn out new code, because they aren't getting hung up on fixing bugs with an underlying framework or trying to decipher a monster 1,000-line method. Being able to focus mostly on new applications or functionality keeps developers feeling productive and fulfilled.

Another beneficial tactic to keep the team happy is to encourage the team to use a set time during the workweek to learn new skills or technologies (as little as an hour, as much as a day). Management will frequently scoff at this, because they don't want to see valuable development time spent on non-work. But there are multiple benefits to be had from this, resulting in a better end product and happier management. Being able to explore a new topic that interests the developer may be rewarding enough to keep them motivated to produce their best work. If it turns out to be something that can benefit the entire team, the developer can present their findings to the others, and the end product may improve too. Using new technologies often inspires developers, and management gets some new buzzwords to use in advertising the product.

Another motivational technique can also make management cringe: *you absolutely must establish that you prioritize quality over quantity.* When developers are encouraged to get projects done quickly, no matter what it takes, the end result is often incredibly sloppy coding and design, and you'll end up paying for it down the line. Want to enhance your product and add new functionality a year later? Guess what—it's now going to take longer to accomplish. The spaghetti-like code may have made sense to the developer(s) working on it at the time, but it's almost guaranteed to require a great deal of study a year later in order to make sense of what it does, whether or not the original developers are still on staff. Your team has to focus on untangling the code before they can even begin to write a single line of a new feature. Focusing on quality up-front, at the cost of extra development time, almost certainly ensures dividends that make up for cost several times over time. Developers are motivated by producing quality work today that they're proud to stand behind, and they will spend less mind-numbing time reworking a poor product in the future.

Overall, creating high standards for your team keeps your developers doing what most developers like doing best—creating new things. When they're producing high-quality work and feeling happy, management is happy as well!

Roy's analysis

This note contains lots of great nuggets. Let's try to analyze why these ideas are good ideas, and why they could be effective in making a team better. We'll analyze this based on the six influence factors model, and in the context of the three team modes.

Coding standard

Setting this guideline affects the social ability and social motivation influence forces:

- *Social ability* means that it'll be socially difficult to behave outside the standard, assuming everyone else is using the standard. When you get into an elevator, you'd find it difficult to face the opposite way when everyone's facing the door.
- *Social motivation* means that if the people you respect and follow on the team adhere to the coding standard, you're likely to think it wise to do the same.

Dedicated learning time

Setting these guidelines affects the environmental ability and motivation influence forces:

- *Environmental ability* means that you're physically able to take time to learn new skills. Many developers don't feel they have time, or they'll be berated by managers for taking the time to learn new things.

- *Environmental motivation* means the company might reward (or at least not punish) you for taking the time to learn. Celebrating developers' achievements in learning new skills, by their managers, would help a great deal. Tying bonuses to learning achievements can help as well, although you might find that sometimes money corrupts the pure nature of loving to learn. You're better off rewarding with symbolic gestures (trophies, awards, and T-shirts) rather than money.

Prioritize quality over quantity

Here we arrive at the real elephant in the room. Quality-over-quantity is one of those "holy grails" that many leaders believe in but have a hard time advocating. The thought's good and pure: we want to affect the environmental motivation influence force to reward people for quality and discourage the opposite. Easier said than done, but there are ways to go about it. Lots of the topics in this book can help. At the end of the day, it takes courage to stand up for the things you believe in. Sometimes it takes guerrilla warfare.

I make sure my estimates contain the quality built-in. For example, I don't say, "It'll be X days total, and X+3 days with testing." My X is always inclusive of testing, TDD, coaching, and pairing time. I don't mention it because it's part of the work. I also don't mention how much of the time I'll spend debugging. That'd be ridiculous. Yet we treat writing tests, pairing, or coaching differently than debugging, when all of these things are facets of the same important work. We allow those who don't understand the work to tell us how to do the work. This is the stand that must be taken, even if quietly, to start making a difference here.

I believe the fault of many projects' horrible quality lies not in the managers, for they know not what they do when they ask for "skipping the testing." It lies with us, the developers, the coders, the testers. We're the ones who should be judged when quality is diluted, because we're the ones who allowed alien hands to smudge the quality that we're responsible for.

That isn't to say that great quality is always the standard. Short-lived code doesn't need tests, if it's only designed to be shown in demos to see if you're even on the right track. If it's *adapted* to become long-lived code, there's no excuse for failing to bring quality back to the forefront and becoming fully responsible for it again.

◆ ◆ ◆ ◆ ◆

DEREK SLAWSON has a natural inclination toward best practices and learning new things. He uses lessons learned through the art of improvisation to provide workshops to organizations that wish to increase the effectiveness of their teams.

25

Stop doing their work

by Brian Dishaw

Chances are you were put into a leadership position because you were good at your previous job. Continuing this behavior as the leader, however, is a dereliction of your current responsibilities. In other words, this means you aren't focusing on learning and growing in your current position. In addition, you're taking away opportunities for your team to learn and grow in their positions. Worst of all, you're actively building a team that has an absence of trust, a lack of accountability, and low commitment to their responsibilities.

> I was promoted as lead developer of a team I had been a developer on from day one. I helped build the system from the ground up and had intimate knowledge of its more complicated and critical subsystems. This worked well when my job was to build the system.

> I quickly identified what needed to happen. I understood the history of the way the system was built (within reach if not within my head), and deciding direction and impact came without much effort. The team of 4 grew to a team of 30 (over the course of a year or so), and then, shortly after, I was promoted.

Soon enough, things ground to a halt. I found myself wondering why as I spent my days putting out fire after fire, cleaning up after my developers. Retrospective after retrospective, the team would push back by saying things like, "Brian's never around," "Brian's too busy to help me, and it's taking me longer than I expected to complete this work," and "Brian's always in meetings."

It didn't take long for the situation to further decay because of my poor reaction to what they were saying; I took it literally. I stayed around more, and I made sure I was visible when I couldn't be actually present. I told people I trusted what to build, only to have to swoop in and clean up something later. The quality of the product deteriorated quickly, and velocity was virtually glacial. I never helped the team with their real problems with ownership, accountability, and trust. I didn't even realize what I'd done to that team until six months after leaving for a different team within the same company.

I can reflect now that what they were really saying wasn't, "Brian's never around," or "Brian's always in meetings." It was, "Brian doesn't trust us. I need to make sure I get his sign-off before I continue."

That one statement sums up three of the common dysfunctions of a team:

- Absence of trust
- Lack of accountability
- Low commitment to the project

This atmosphere developed not because I didn't trust them or didn't want them to be successful, but because I took their growth opportunities from them. I failed to learn how to be an effective leader. The irony is I had previously been the catalyst for a healthy velocity of the product, only to turn around and, as team leader, make it grind to a halt. Had I realized then what I know now, things could've been better for that team. It still would've been difficult to let go of complete control, but every time I slipped I would've had something to fall back on that I could try again.

Roy's analysis

I believe this note depicts a classic case of a team leader who, for one reason or another, keeps their team out of learning mode. Another way to interpret this is that you'll get bad behaviors if you treat a learning team or a self-organizing team as if they were in survival mode.

Acting as a command-and-control leader when being a coach fits the current situation brings poor results. Being "command and control" with a self-organizing team is disastrous.

◆ ◆ ◆ ◆ ◆

BRIAN DISHAW is a leader who embraces failure and uses experiences to empower, teach, and grow others.

26

Write code, but not too much

by Patrick Kua

I have worked with many team leaders, and one of the most difficult activities is balancing time spent writing code with other leadership activities. In an extreme case, writing no code leads to a lack of specific context for any direction you might want push the team. Even with the most positive of intents, without grounding in a system's current state, any decisions you make might cause more work than needed. In the other extreme case, writing too much code probably means other important leadership activities are being neglected and any broader technical issues remain unresolved.

Circumstances often dictate the time you have to code. Your leadership role means representation in many more meetings. Time in meetings will pull you away from writing code. You'll also find some of these meetings more ad hoc, making any coding effort difficult to do without interruption.

I've found that accommodating and balancing a team leader's coding needs is easiest in teams practicing pair programming, as long as they also practice frequent rotation and collective code ownership. The idea is that you can work with your partner to design a solution, or, at least, agree on a direction to take for solving a problem. If you find yourself dragged off to meetings, then any functionality being built or changed doesn't stop being developed, and you can rejoin with only a slight interruption to progress. Your team still enjoys the benefits of your specific knowledge about the code base, while you care for the other activities your role requires of you.

For teams who don't practice pair programming, any time you find for coding is best spent on tasks away from the critical path, particularly if it's likely to block others from completing their work. For some people, this might be a scary idea, but you need to have trust in the team, or at least ensure the team has the right mix of skills to tackle critical issues. Great team leaders delegate tasks early and have frequent design or code reviews to ensure overall standards are met.

Team leaders should seek critical technical debt that continually drags at the team, and look for ways to break down large chunks into smaller, more manageable chunks.

As tempting as it is for team leaders to take all the interesting stuff, teams excel when their leaders remove impediments and let the team work out the best way to get stuff done.

Roy's analysis

This note is thoughtful. I agree with many things said here. Let's take this note one step further, to the next level of leadership. What happens after you've implemented this note? The team performs nicely, but they still *need* you to be there, or everything goes to pieces. How can we alleviate that and move the team to true self-organization?

Whatever it is you're doing that makes you unique and irreplaceable as a team leader is a burden that turns you into a bus factor. Teach those skills to the team to make yourself replaceable, and they can self-organize. For example, detecting important technical debt that holds people back is a skill that can be taught. Break up big problems into smaller problems—people can be coached to learn the ideas and detection techniques behind this.

If you agree that a leader's job is to *always* remove impediments, then you've reduced their job to a snow shovel. I believe a leader's job is to remove impediments *during survival mode,* teach the team how to remove impediments during *learning mode,* and watch as the team removes impediments in *self-organizing mode.*

◆   ◆   ◆   ◆   ◆

PATRICK KUA works as an active, generalizing specialist for ThoughtWorks and dislikes being put into a box. He's the author of the book *Talking with Tech Leads* (CreateSpace Independent Publishing Platform, 2015). Patrick is often found leading technical teams, coaching people and organizations in lean and agile methods, and facilitating situations beyond adversity. He's fascinated by elements of learning and continuous improvement, always helping others to develop enthusiasm for these same elements. You can find out more about him at www.thekua.com/atwork/.

27

Evolving from manager to leader

by Tricia Broderick

Dear Tricia of 2000,

This year seemed like the logical choice to select. Professionally, you've successfully managed several small projects and have received numerous recognitions.

Personally, you got engaged and, most importantly, Michigan State University won the national basketball title! So your awesome mood coupled with your next assignment, managing your first 30-person team, should make you fairly receptive to this message.

I know well how much you pride yourself on being highly dependable. Yet, I also know that, as a manager, you struggle with feeling out of control. Your solution is to engage in hands-on risk mitigation. You convince yourself this is in everyone's best interest, as the task needs to get done and you're simply setting an example, coaching others on how to avoid problems.

The flaw in this logic will be missed for years because you'll have good success both in customer delivery and group dynamics. I can already hear you asking, "Exactly where's the problem?"

Are you really okay with results that are merely good, or do you want awesome results for yourself and your teams? That's what I thought; humor me, and keep reading.

Being a manager will produce good results, but evolving into a leader who's also capable as a manager will produce empowered teams that achieve awesome results. No, don't argue with me; not only are you *not* a leader today, you won't be able to change immediately and become a leader tomorrow.

Your evolution from a manager to a leader will be primarily based on a combination of two assets:

- Your ability to adapt and handle any risk or issue. Your high dependability isn't a result of problems never occurring, but how you're able to effectively minimize impacts and use opportunities appropriately.
- Your passion and skill for coaching and mentoring. You've already experienced that people appreciate it when you invest in helping them grow.

You're lucky—adapting and the desire to help others come naturally to you, but there's a catch; to be aware and possess these assets won't be enough. Until now, you've often relied on other core traits that have prevented teams from being empowered.

Perfection vs. learning

Specifically, you need to dampen your desires for being the go-to expert and for perfection. For example, you've already learned that responding to a problem on the team with, "I should fix that myself," won't scale.

But you've only adjusted the response to, "What didn't I teach them to avoid this problem?" which means that you expected your team to excel *through your help.*

Now don't go over-analyzing with a thousand examples of why they could've avoided a problem. There absolutely is a time and a place for coaching—this relates to the important aspect of being a capable manager. The leader mindset, which requires a response of, "How can I help them learn and adapt from this?" needs to be your first impulse. Your focus has to be on creating an environment that's dedicated to helping teams and individuals become adaptive, learning-focused, and cohesive.

Trust

There's no sugar coating how much work it takes to become a leader. You must maintain the skills necessary to effectively manage. At the same time, begin with work that builds trust both ways to empower people. This will be the easier part, given that your integrity and intentions are pretty visible, and you have no problem interacting with people.

The trick is to remember that numerous situations are usually required before you'll trust that they can adapt and, more importantly, that they fully believe you trust them to adapt.

Failure

Tackle the challenging work that drives you crazy; embrace failure as a learning opportunity despite knowing it can be prevented. You must always keep in mind that your perspective should be on the team, what's best for their growth even when you and/or they might look bad in the process.

Results

I realize the devil's advocate in you probably wonders whether all of this work is worth the difference in results. Without any hesitation, the answer is yes! You'll experience team results that exceed your highest expectations. You'll find yourself more engaged at work with the challenges you now face.

Satisfaction

The factor that makes the answer obvious is the satisfaction you get from helping others. The recognition you receive today pales in comparison to that which you'll experience as a leader. I still smile when I think about the time my team surprised me with an appreciation award. People stood up and made these types of statements: "I appreciate the way she pushes me out of my comfort zone in a way that makes me feel supported," to "I appreciate how she calls me out on my BS," all the way to "I appreciate her helping to pick out gifts for my wife." I couldn't help but walk out of that conference room proud of my team, and, consequently, proud of myself too, because I helped create an environment that I want to work and play hard in every day. That's worth everything!

—From your future self, Tricia of 2016

Roy's analysis

This note comes from a highly experienced manager and leader, and it discusses a subtlety I've barely touched on in this book: what is coaching in the context of elastic leadership?

Tricia used to think coaching meant teaching teams the right techniques to avoid future mistakes, with the goal of making mistakes ultimately (hopefully) disappear.

The lesson she gradually learned is that growing a team means a learning process has to happen, and learning happens when you tackle things out of your comfort zone, where the chance of making mistakes is *higher*, not lower.

The paradox here is that by only teaching the team techniques to avoid failure, Tricia denied the team true learning and growth opportunities. Yes, they know how to do something, but do they know what to do when things go wrong? When things don't work? Who do they turn to when that happens? Do they turn to themselves and have the skills to deal without knowing what to do next? Or do they need Tricia, who's now the bus factor of "I'm stuck" situations?

When I teach my kids to ride a bicycle, I expect them to fall. I don't expect to teach them so perfectly that they won't fall at the beginning. Once they can ride in the most basic way, I expect (and fear) they'll start exploring what they can do with a bicycle. Can they jump over obstacles? Can they go up ramps? Can they ride backwards? They'll experiment and find their own way.

I can't teach my kids how to be ultimately successful with people. I can give them some initial tools, but I expect them to experiment and fail and learn what it's like to live among other humans. I also expect misery and sadness and joy and happiness, and it'd be terrible of me to keep them in a safe bubble where everyone they ever meet always behaves the way my kids expect them to behave.

Coaching isn't only the act of holding a hand; it's the act of letting go, even briefly. It's the acting of helping when they fail and asking, "What can you learn from this?" Sometimes leadership isn't about being there, but about removing yourself from the equation, albeit temporarily.

In the context of team modes and leadership styles, *survival mode* calls for hand-holding, *learning mode* calls for alternating between hand-holding and letting go, and *self-organization* calls for letting go and watching from a safe distance—not so far that you can't help out if the team reverts to one of the other modes.

◆ ◆ ◆ ◆ ◆

TRICIA BRODERICK is one of the directors of development at TechSmith. Tricia is responsible for creating and maintaining an engaging and empowering environment for software engineering teams to deliver high-quality products. With 16 years of experience, the last 6 of which focused on agile principles, her passion for mentoring and coaching has been essential in successfully transitioning from a manager to an agile leader.

Recently, her team summarized her leadership by highlighting that she knows when to honestly challenge someone out of their comfort zone while consistently providing support and encouragement.

28

Affecting the pace of change

by Tom Howlett

I'm in a lucky and rare position to have been with the same team for more than 10 years (more than half of the original team remains, although we are all greatly changed). In that time, we've come from chaos to self-organizing—the team is happy and effective and constantly challenges the status quo. We're proud of what we've achieved. I think our only regret is we didn't get there faster. Luckily, you've got the wisdom in this book to help you achieve that.

Why so long?

Ten years is a long time, more time than most teams get to become effective before they are outsourced. Why did it take so long? Agile development is all about shortening feedback loops. Perhaps, if we'd done feedback more aggressively, it might have helped, but on the other hand, too much feedback too soon can be overwhelming, causing anxiety and building walls. To facilitate change as a leader, you need to learn techniques to encourage others to adopt change while remaining a happy and effective team.

Team-based ideas

Ideas for change should come from within the team as well as from you. They come from reflection on what's not right, and inspiration from other teams. Encourage the team to network at user groups, read blogs, and use Twitter and other social media. These resources make a huge difference to a team's enthusiasm for change.

Consensus

For change to be successfully adopted, a team needs to have consensus. As a team lead, it's your job to ensure consensus is built; retrospectives, stand-ups, or spontaneous chats are where it happens. Ensure these happen when necessary and are done in environments conducive to constructive dialogue. If you want to run these well, it's worth learning facilitation techniques from books like Jean Tabaka's *Collaboration Explained: Facilitation Skills for Software Project Leaders* (Addison-Wesley Professional, 2006).

Personalities

Your team will undoubtedly comprise different personality types. Some will focus on getting things done, some will look at the details, and some will find creative solutions to difficult problems. This will cause tension. In the early days, the tension creates anxiety and frustration, but as collaboration improves, this tension contributes to effectiveness. The key to making this transition is to encourage the team to value each other's strengths and understand that, combined, these strengths will help each member to become stronger.

Conflict

If you're continually improving, there will be conflict. If there isn't, it's a good warning sign that you're stagnating. It's important to every team member that they're respected for being competent at their job. New ideas that challenge the way they currently work have the potential to challenge their feeling of competence, leading to embarrassment. Our brains put up strong defenses to avoid this, particularly at first. Don't become frustrated; be sensitive, but don't let defensiveness stop you.

Barricades

If a discussion starts going in circles with multiple people pushing their opinions and you can't see a way out, draw the meeting to a close. Don't be despondent, and look to find out why. Take time to talk to people individually, but remain their equal in the conversation. Look at the work of Chris Argyris to ensure you get the most out of these conversations (check out the resources section on Benjamin Mitchell's blog at http://blog.benjaminm.net/argyris/). Ask questions, and spend as much time inquiring into their cause as you do in advocating yours. If it doesn't work, give it another day or two and talk again. In advocating your cause, explain the evidence that backs up the need to change, and explain and question your assumptions. When trying to understand their point of view, try to find out the evidence and assumptions they used to reach their conclusions. With practice, you can use these techniques during the first meeting.

Pace

Attempt to find a pace of change that doesn't cause anxiety to team members. Using the discussed techniques can make change faster and smoother. Don't become disheartened; change takes time. Give others time, but ensure you are helping the process as much as you can.

Roy's analysis

One idea that this note touches on, that's covered somewhat in chapter 4, is *pace*. At what *pace* do we want change to occur? Do we always want change to happen quickly? Is there a downside to that?

The note demonstrates several levers you can pull to move things along—to increase pace. But taking longer to make changes isn't always a bad idea. Too many changes in parallel can create an environment that feels unstable. If you're dealing with people who've been in the same place for 10 or 20 years, this could be too disruptive, and you might lose some good people.

In other organizations, a fast pace of change might be a great idea, and there's no time like the present. Either way, considering *pace* might be something you want to plan as a change agent in your organization.

The author claims that consensus is needed for change to happen. I'd say, "Yes, sometimes." It depends on the current mode the team is in. In survival mode, the team might not be a part of the decision-making process when changes are necessary. In fact, sometimes teams in survival mode don't even know what the right decision might be. That's how they got into survival mode. When the team is in learning mode, you might want to push them to *try* to get consensus, but only as part of a learning exercise—"How do we get consensus among ourselves as a team of peers?" Not all decisions will be greeted with acceptance. As an Israeli, I can tell you any decision that doesn't have at least two dissenters in a team of eight people isn't a meaningful decision. Conflict is important.

On the other hand, everyone needs to be *heard*. Then a decision can be made, even if everyone's not on board. People who have been *heard* can feel committed to do things they don't agree with, as long as they said everything they wanted to say, and they know it was considered. As long as you end up with "We considered this feedback, and we're going to go with X anyway," people can still follow the decision.

Perhaps *partial* consensus might be a better fit in some situations. Remember that learning mode is about getting out of your comfort zone, and that sometimes means executing decisions you're not comfortable with. I sometimes tell new team leads, "If everyone's happy in your team all the time, you're doing something wrong. You're not pushing anyone out of their comfort zone." Perhaps a *lack* of consensus is a sign of a learning team. As the note said, conflict *is* good. Don't expect to be able to fix all conflicts.

The last part of the note deals with barricading. Trying to convince a team member of something they disagree with can be frustrating. This is where the six influence forces come in handy.

Usually we only look at personal motivation and personal ability. Can I explain logically why this is a good idea? Can the team physically follow the idea? With the influence forces, we can look at four more possible reasons why that person isn't on board with our ideas for change. Maybe the company reward system rewards the opposite behavior. Maybe people they respect do the opposite of what we propose.

Time to research!

◆ ◆ ◆ ◆ ◆

TOM HOWLETT has been developing web applications using Microsoft technologies for the last 15 years with a particular enthusiasm for Agile principles, Scrum, and Kanban. He spent the last 5 years as a Scrum master and enjoys blogging about the experience here: http://diaryofascrummaster .wordpress.com.

29

Proximity management

by Jurgen Appelo

When I started working as a manager, I had my own big office with a shiny desk, a new, fast computer, and a desk phone with more buttons than the ceremonial suit of your average dictator. I also had a workforce of a dozen software developers, to do with as I pleased. I lacked one thing: I had no clue how to be a manager.

When I investigated my "communication issue," I realized its solution involved proximity. Sitting side-by-side in the same room is more effective than having two people sit in private adjacent offices.

The first approach: move your behind

When you understand that distance reduces communication, you can try to optimize communication by optimizing proximity. The suggestions on *how* to do this differ in detail, but they all boil down to the same thing: the manager should move away from their desk, toward the important work.

The advice is often presented under the Japanese name *Gemba*, which says the manager ought to be there where the work happens in order to understand how healthy the organization is and to help solve any problems people might have, using facts and not assumptions.

Other names you may find are *Genchi Genbutsu, Go and See,* and *Management by Walking Around (MBWA).* In the case of distributed teams, this could become *Management by Flying Around (MBFA).*

The second approach: move your desk

Years ago I realized the concept of "being where the work happens" can be taken a step further. I solved it by picking up my stuff to sit with my team at a normal desk. This allowed me to absorb more of what was going on. People spontaneously asked for my opinion and I picked up signs of joy and frustration, which I wouldn't have noticed if I hadn't been there.

When there are more teams involved, you can combine the two techniques according to two proximity principles:

- *Distance to people should match importance of work.* See what your teams are working on or how they work, and sit with the team that needs special attention.
- *Diversity in distance should match diversity of work.* Optimize your communication with others by walking around. There should be diversity in your distance to people, which depends on the diversity of their locations and their work.

Whatever you do, go to the problems. Don't wait for problems to find you.

Roy's analysis

In the larger context of this book, this note deals with one of the influence forces: environmental ability. By moving closer to where the important things are, you have more *ability* to notice and react to things faster.

You change your environment to better enable behaviors from yourself as a manager, and from your team, by making yourself more approachable.

◆ ◆ ◆ ◆ ◆

Jurgen Appelo Since 2008, Jurgen has been writing a popular blog at www.noop.nl, which deals with development management, software engineering, business improvement, personal development, and complexity theory. He's the author of the book *Management 3.0: Leading Agile Developers, Developing Agile Leaders* (Addison Wesley Professional, 2001), which describes the role of the manager in agile organizations. He also authored the book *How to Change the World* (Jojo Ventures BV, 2012), which describes his new supermodel for change management.

30

Babel Fish

by Gil Zilberfeld

I don't remember much from my first day as a team leader. It could be I was entranced with being anointed with a title someone else had left behind, or simply because it was many years ago.

Since then, I've learned many things that I should've done on that fateful day and in the following years. I didn't realize it then, but on that day I became a Babel Fish. For those who don't recognize the term, a Babel Fish is a fictitious animal from Douglas Adams' books, which performs instant translations. That wasn't on the job description. As a new team leader, communication and translation of information is your most crucial role, and from now on your task is to improve as a Babel Fish.

A team leader needs to communicate through multiple channels

Up, down, and sideways—information about business requirements and needs, risk, and stability issues—this all needs to be communicated to interested parties. Suppose a new business requirement is added to the project. Your team can work off a spec, but it's better if you communicate the motivation behind that requirement, in a language that the team understands. Perhaps the team identifies a risk when implementing the requirement. You can update the status to, "We'll be late by two weeks, sorry," but it would be more effective to communicate the reason behind the delay, in a language business people understand. Most professionals in a field don't understand that specialists in another field don't speak their language. Team leaders provide translation services to ensure everyone heads in the right direction. That's you, buddy!

Awareness is the first step. The next step's harder: to become a successful Babel Fish, you need to learn more languages than you now know. That means business language, technical language, tester language, marketing language, sales language, HR language. In order to do that, you need to go out, converse, and learn.

Get out of the development silo, and talk to other humans. It isn't easy, but it's worth it.

In addition to your team benefiting from better information, including the "why do this" factor, you get a bonus: better relationships with people from other departments. You'll need it in order to improve your team. Imagine what it'd be like if the HR guy let you skip a few forms when you interview a star you don't want to miss out on. You can benefit your team outside the confines of the project by having trusting relationships with everyone else. If you make this your priority, everything else will fall in line. To better communicate with your team, you'll need to talk with them more. This way, you'll know how to improve their effectiveness and challenge them with the tasks that benefit them. Your team will earn respect because they have a team leader normal people can talk with. It's like relationship inheritance. Most of all, you'll grow as a person, as a team leader, and as a communicator. As everyone knows, it's all about communication.

Congratulations on your new job, Babel Fish!

Roy's analysis

From the perspective of the influence forces, this note deals with the personal motivation aspect. A Babel Fish is a translator, which means they understand how to say things to the other side of the equation in a way that matters to *the other side*. Understanding what marketing folks care about and speaking on the same level with them shows that you empathize with them enough to learn their language.

Yes, this is politics. Good politics leave everyone better off in the long run.

Another interesting observation is that, in our Team Leader Manifesto, we emphasize working with people and understanding humans at least as much as we do machines, because all problems are people problems at their root. In my mind, a Babel Fish is someone who's mastered the art of understanding where the other side's coming from and can put themselves in their shoes. It's a priceless skill to have, and I urge everyone to master it.

◆ ◆ ◆ ◆ ◆

GIL ZILBERFELD has been in software since childhood, starting out with Logo turtles. With almost 20 years of developing commercial software under his belt, he has vast experience in software methodology and practices. Gil is the product manager at Typemock, working as part of an agile team in an agile company, creating tools for agile developers. He promotes unit testing and other design best practices, down-to-earth agile methods, and incredibly cool tools. He speaks in local and international venues about unit testing, TDD, and agile practices and communication. And in his spare time, he shoots zombies for fun. Gil blogs at www.gilzilberfeld.com on different agile topics, including processes, communication, and unit testing.

31

You're the lead, not the know-it-all

by Johanna Rothman

One of the traps team leads encounter is the need to know it all. It doesn't matter if you're a team lead of 3 people or 30 people; you became a team lead because of your technical skill, right? That must mean you're pretty smart, and you're supposed to lead, right? You're supposed to have lots of great ideas. You're supposed to know lots of things. You're supposed to be able to solve lots of problems. Well, that doesn't mean you have to solve every problem yourself.

Many years ago, when I was a technical lead, I was also the project manager. We were a three-person project. I was the team lead, Andy was my junior person, and Mark was my mechanical engineer. We were working on a machine vision project back in the mid-1980s, when cameras were able to collect up to eight bits of data per pixel. That's not megabits; that's only eight bits.

Andy and I were working on the software for gauge inspection. Mark helped us by creating the gauge holder. Yes, it took three to implement this project. The gauges were similar to the gas gauges or mileage gauges in cars back in the '80s; they were orange lines against black backgrounds with other white markings at regular intervals. Our job was to detect the angle of the orange line on the gauge.

With today's cameras, this isn't a difficult problem. With the cameras of 1984, the problem was huge. We needed to light the gauge precisely. We needed to know if we were picking up the orange line, not the white markings. With only 8 bits per pixel, and the computing power back in 1984, you can imagine our problems.

I'd started developing the algorithms and asked Andy to continue, but the calculations weren't 100% reliable. We were doing a code review when Mark asked about the gauge holder. He listened for a minute and asked some questions, and soon we were discussing whether the gauge holder should hold the gauges sideways or straight up.

I no longer remember the resolution, but I do remember the power of the discussion. When I relinquished power as the *only* technical lead, everyone's problem-solving skills came to the fore. Everyone engaged in solving the problem. Everyone grew excited.

We finished that project successfully. I suspect Andy's solution won, which is why I no longer remember, but that's the value of technical leadership—to facilitate the team to the *best* solution, not *your* solution.

Did I know it all? No. Did I know enough? Yes. I knew enough to start problem-solving and facilitate the rest of the team.

Team leadership isn't about knowing everything and doling out information and solutions. Team leadership is about creating an environment in which everyone can flourish to the best of each person's ability—including you.

Loosen the reins on your team. You, too, will grow and flourish. That's the lesson I learned.

Roy's analysis

This powerful note, in the greater context of this book, deals with a couple of ideas.

Being the bus factor

By establishing yourself as the sole tech lead, you become the main bottleneck for decision-making. You also turn into a bus factor. Without you, the team can't function, which is a huge risk. Yes, technically maybe they *could* function, but they might grow afraid to function without you because they're used to you approving all decisions. If you're gone for a week, things will slow to a crawl in the decision-making space. This is also an example of the environmental motivation influence force at work. People will feel less comfortable making decisions because they think their leader expects them not to make decisions on their own, which might hurt their career.

Coaching vs. command-and-control leadership

Not only are you becoming a bus factor, you're also not coaching, but "telling." If your team wants to learn new things, or feels they could handle making decisions without you, but you keep insisting on your own ideas, that might fly for a while during survival mode; but in learning and self-organization modes, you'll start losing people fast.

◆　◆　◆　◆　◆

JOHANNA ROTHMAN, author of the *Pragmatic Manager* newsletter, helps organizational leaders see problems and risks in their product development, seize opportunities, and remove impediments. She's the author of several management and project management books. You can read more about Johanna and find her blogs and her writings at www.jrothman.com.

32

Actions speak louder than words

by Dan North

The way you act says more about your values than any pithy motivational slogan. A team is more likely to follow your lead in terms of your behavior than they are to follow your instructions, particularly if these aren't aligned.

If you talk about valuing feedback and then get defensive when someone offers some, the team will unconsciously pick up on the defensive behavior. Conversely, if you always take the time to check in with your team, they'll get into the habit of telling you things and may even become more comfortable talking with one another. Sometimes, this modelling can have a surprising upside, when you notice the team picking up a behavior intrinsic enough to your values that you never thought to make it explicit.

One of the toughest starts I had as a software team leader involved joining a team of nine strongly opinionated developers as their lead. They'd formed cliques within the team, and each thought the others were idiots and didn't understand software. I was brought in primarily as facilitator: an external person who wasn't vested in any of the cliques and who might be able to help them find a way forward.

My first priority was to take each member of the team out for coffee, one at a time, away from the office, and listen. I asked each person the same questions: what they liked and what frustrated them about the team, the software, and the project, and what they wanted to change. The thing that surprised me most was that they all saw the same issues and wanted to make almost the same changes. Before I got there, the team decided to introduce a design change to make part of the code more understandable, and they were busy arguing about how to implement it. There were some differences in the details, and it was here that cliques were forming. It seemed to me this was more about jostling for position than about an objectively better or worse technical solution.

I used the Shackleton technique of asking everyone for their input and then making a decision, while actively engaging with and listening to dissenters. We went ahead with one of the options; after a couple of weeks, we realized it wasn't helping, and, in fact, the whole approach was making things worse! I took the responsibility for a bad decision, and we backed out the change, cleaning up as we went. Then a strange thing happened: people started to become less defensive and began experimenting a little. I inadvertently demonstrated that it was okay to try something and fail, which unlocked a whole new style of working.

If the boss could admit a mistake and move on, perhaps admitting uncertainty wasn't such a sign of weakness after all. In fact, for a time the pendulum swung the other way, with people proudly announcing how little they knew about something, but that they were still willing to give it a go! Over time, it settled into a healthy rhythm of trying out several ideas, evaluating them, and then deciding which ones to progress. Rather than taking an absolute position and defending it, the team members became more open to the idea of discourse and collaboration, valuing team learning over their own individual status.

Roy's analysis

In influence forces terms, this note deals with social motivation and environmental motivation.

People tend to imitate people they respect. If I see someone in the team whom I highly respect do something, like make mistakes and admit them publicly, and then see that nothing bad happens, I might be less afraid to confess my own mistakes and know that there will be no environmental punishment for it.

If I do that, and then my team leader comes to me and says, "Great job experimenting!" that's an environmental reward: it's reasonable to assume that my job is safer because my manager likes what I do, so I'm more likely to repeat the behavior.

Actions speak louder than words because they imply social motivation ("I'm not the only one"). Environmental motivation is implied if the organization rewards and appreciates those who make mistakes while trying to experiment.

❖ ❖ ❖ ❖ ❖

DAN NORTH is an independent technology consultant who writes software and coaches teams and organizations in Agile and Lean methods. He believes in putting people first and writing simple, pragmatic software.

index

Soft Skills
The software developer's life manual
by John Z. Sonmez

ISBN: 9781617292392
5048 pages
$34.99
December 2014

Kanban in Action
by Marcus Hammarberg and Joakim Sundén

ISBN: 9781617291050
360 pages
$44.99
February 2014

Specification by Example
How Successful Teams Deliver the Right Software
by Gojko Adzic

ISBN: 9781617290084
296 pages
$49.99
June 2011

For ordering information go to www.manning.com

The Art of Unit Testing, Second Edition
with examples in C#
by Roy Osherove

ISBN: 9781617290893
296 pages
$44.99
November 2013

Agile Metrics in Action
How to measure and improve team performance
by Christopher W. H. Davis

ISBN: 9781617292484
272 pages
$44.99
July 2015

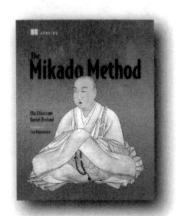

The Mikado Method
by Ola Ellnestam and Daniel Brolund

ISBN: 9781617291210
240 pages
$44.99
March 2014

For ordering information go to www.manning.com